FLORENTINE CODEX

Florentine Codex

General History of the Things of New Spain

FRAY BERNARDINO DE SAHAGÚN

Book 8 – Kings and Lords

Translated from the Aztec into English, with notes and illustrations

By

ARTHUR J. O. ANDERSON
SCHOOL OF AMERICAN RESEARCH

CHARLES E. DIBBLE
UNIVERSITY OF UTAH

IN THIRTEEN PARTS

PART IX

Chapter heading designs are from the Codex

Published by

The School of American Research and The University of Utah

Monographs of The School of American Research

Number 14, Part IX   Santa Fe, New Mexico   1979

Published and distributed by
The University of Utah Press
Salt Lake City, Utah

CONTENTS

EIGHTH BOOK

LIST OF ILLUSTRATIONS

following page 36

BOOK EIGHT--KINGS AND LORDS

Libro octauo, de los
Reyes, y señores, y de
la manera: que teni
an, en sus electio
nes: y en el goui
erno de sus
Reinos.

De los Reyes

EIGHTH BOOK, WHICH TELLETH OF THE GREAT RULERS AND NOBLEMEN AND OF THE WAY IN WHICH THEY OBSERVED THE ELECTIONS IN THEIR GOVERNMENT.

JNIC CHICUEI AMOXTLI INTECHPA TLATOA YN HUEHUEY TLATOQUE IOAN IN PIPILTI YOAN IN QUENIN QUIPIAIA TLAPEPENALIZTLI YN IPAN TLATOCAIOTL.

First Chapter, which telleth of the rulers and governors who reigned in Mexico from the beginning of [their] rule until the year 1560.

Inic ce capitulo itechpa tlatoa in tlatoque ioan in gouernadores in otlatocatque mexico in isquichica ipeuhcan tlatocaiotl ioan in ixquichica xihuitl de 1560.

The first ruler of Mexico.

Acamapichtli first made the beginning, and ruled Tenochtitlan twenty-one years. There was peace and quiet; wars had not yet come in his reign.

Inic ce mexico tlatoani

Acamapichtli achto compeoalti tlatocat in tenochtitlan cempoalxiuitl oce iuian iocoxca in catca, aiatle iaoiotl ipan mochiuh.

The second ruler of Tenochtitlan.

Uitziliuitl was second, and ruled Tenochtitlan twenty-one years. He began wars and conquered the people of Colhuacan.

Inic ome tenochtitlã tlatoanj.

Vitzilihuitl ic ome tlatocat in tenochtitlan cempoalxiuitl oçe iehoatl quipeoalti in iauiotl, quinpeuh in colhoacan tlaca.

The third ruler of Tenochtitlan.

Chimalpopoca was third. He ruled Tenochtitlan ten years.

Ic ei tenochtitlan tlatoani.

Chimalpopoca ic ei tlatocat in tenochtitlan matlacxiuitl.

The fourth ruler of Tenochtitlan.

Itzcoatzin was fourth, and ruled Tenochtitlan fourteen years. He conquered the people of Azcapotzalco and Xochimilco.

Ic naui tenochtitlan tlatoani.

Itzcoatzin ic naui tlatocat in tenochtitlan matlacxiuitl onnaui qujnpeuh in azcaputzalca ioan xuchmilca

The fifth ruler of Tenochtitlan.

Moctezuma the Elder was fifth, and ruled Tenochtitlan thirty years. He conquered and made war on all the people of Chalco; and on Quauhnauac and on all who were subject to Quauhnauac; and on Maçauacan. And in his reign there came a great

Inic macuilli tenochtitlan tlatoani

Veue motecuçoma, ic macuilli tlatocat in tenochtitlan: cempoalxiujtl ipan matlacxiuitl, quipeuh qujiauchiuh in jxqujch chalcatl ioan quauhnaoac ioan in ixquich moquauhnaoacaitoa ioan maçaoacan, ioan ipan mochiuh in vei maianaliztli, nauhxiuitl in

1

famine, which spread over the land for four years. Hence was it said that all were affected by the year One Rabbit. All the people of Mexico, and the Tepaneca and those of Acolhuacan dispersed among other [people].

The sixth ruler of Tenochtitlan.

Axayacatl was the sixth, and ruled Tenochtitlan fourteen years. It came to pass in his reign that there was war between the people of Tlatilulco and those of Tenochtitlan. As a result of the struggle, the reign of Tlatilulco then came to an end. For forty-six years no one else reigned in Tlatilulco. And when the war was waged, he who was ruling Tlatilulco was named Moquiuixtli.

And this Axayacatl conquered Tlacotepec, and Callimaya, and Metepec, Callixtlauacan, Ecatepec, Cozcaquauhtenanco, Teotenanco, Malinaltenanco, Tzinacantepec, Coatepec, Cuitlapilco, Teoxaualco, Tequaloian, and Ocuillan.

The seventh ruler of Tenochtitlan.

Tiçocicatzin was the seventh, and ruled Tenochtitlan four years. No wars were made in his reign.

The eighth ruler of Tenochtitlan.

Auitzotl was the eighth, and he ruled Tenochtitlan for eighteen years. When he was ruler, Mexico was flooded. By his command it was done; five springs were opened, known as Acuecuexatl, Tlillatl, Uitzillatl, Xochcaatl, and Coaatl, which were in the territory of Coyoacan and Uitzilopochco.[1] When Mexico was flooded, four years were still to pass before Auitzotl died. And when the Spaniards came here, it was already twenty-two years before that Mexico had been flooded.

And it came to pass in his time that the sun was eclipsed, at midday. For about five hours the darkness was overspread; the stars appeared. All were much terrified. It was said: "The demons of darkness will descend; they will eat people."

And he conquered those of Tziuhcoac, and Mollanco, Tlapan, Chiapan, Xaltepec, Izoatlan, Xochtlan, Amaxtlan, Mapachtepec, Xoconochco, Ayotlan, Maçatlan, and Coyoacan.

The ninth ruler of Tenochtitlan.

Moctezuma was the ninth, and he ruled Tenoch-

manca injc mjtoa Necetochuiloc tepan moiaoac ɩn jxquich mexicatl ioan tepanecatl, ioan acolhoacatl.

Injc chicoacen, tenochtitlan tlatoani.

Axaiaca ic chicoacen tlatocat in tenochtitlan: matlacxiuitl ipã nauhxiuitl. Ipan mochiuh inic moiaochiuhque tlatilulca, ioan tenochca: inic mjxnamjque, vncan poliuh in tlatocaiotl tlatilulco: vmpoalxiujtl ipan chiquacenxiujtl in aocac tlatocat tlatilulco. Auh in jcoac mochiuh iauiotl: tlatocatia in tlatilulco, itoca moquiuixtli.

Auh in iehoatl axaiaca, qujpeuh in tlacotepec, ioan callimaia, ioan metepec, callixtlaoaca, hecatepec, cozcaquauhtenanco, teutenanco, malinaltenãco, tzinacantepec, coatepec, cujtlapilco, teoxaoalco, tequaloia, ocujllan.

Injc chicome, tenochtitlan tlatoanj.

Tiçoçicatzin, ic chicome tlatocat in tenochtitlan nauhxiujtl. Atle ipan mochiuh in iaviotl.

Injc chicuej, tenochtitlan tlatoanj.

Aujtzotl, ic chicuej tlatocat in tenochtitlan: caxtolxiujtl ipan exiuitl. Icoac tlatocati in apachiuh Mexico: itencopa mochiuh, inic motlapo macujltetl oztotl in jntoca Acuecuexatl, tlillatl, Vitzillatl xochcaatl, coahatl, inma in coioacã ioan ujtzilupuchco: oc nauhxiujtl qujtztia, injc apachiuh mexico, in aiamo mjqui aujtzutl. Auh in jcoac oallaque Españoles, ie iuh cempoalxiujtl omome, oapachiuh in mexico:

ioan ipan mochiuh in tonatiuh qualoc, nepantla tonatiuh: aço macujlli horas in tlaioatimanca, nezque in cicitlalti, cenca nemauhtiloc, mjtoaia: ca oaltemozque in tzitzimime, tequazque:

ioan quinpeuh in tziuhcoaca, ioan mollanco, tlapan, chiapan, xaltepec, izoatlan, xochtlan, amaxtlan, mapachtepec, xoconochco, aiutlan, maçatlan, coioacan.

Injc chicunauj, tlatoanj tenochtitlan.

Motecuçuma ic chicunaui tlatocat in tenochtitlan

---

1. *Inma in coioacã.* The *Real Academia de la Historia MS* has ỹ *mani* for *inma.*

titlan for nineteen years. In his reign there came a famine; for two years[2] it spread over the land, during which it rained no more. Because of it the people of Mexico dispersed everywhere, and there was great suffering from hunger.

In the reign of this same [ruler] it happened that there in the song house which was in Tenochtitlan, a beam, which pierced the walls which held it, sang.[3] It intoned, "Woe, my evil rump! Dance well, for thou shalt be cast into the water!" This came to pass when [the fame of] the Spaniards came to be known.

In the days of this same [ruler] it happened that [the demon] Ciuacoatl went about weeping, at night. Everyone heard it wailing and saying: "My beloved sons, now I am about to leave you."

In the reign of the same [ruler] this came to pass. A woman of quality, whose home was in Tenochtitlan, died of a sickness. She was buried then in her courtyard, and they laid stones over [her grave]. Four days after the dead woman had been buried, she came to life at night. Greatly were all frightened. There, where she had been buried in her grave, it was burst open, and the stones which had been laid over it went to scatter at a distance. And this woman, after she had returned to life, then went to converse and speak with Moctezuma about what she had seen. She informed and said to him: "For this reason have I returned to life: I have come to tell thee that thou art come to the end. With thee the reign of Mexico ceaseth; for in thy time the city of Mexico will end. They who come, lo, these have come to subjugate the land; these will occupy Mexico." And this woman who had died lived another twenty-one years, and once more bore a son.

And many [were] the cities which Moctezuma conquered. Their names [were] Icpatepec, Cuezcomaixtlauacan, Çocollan, Tecomaixtlauacan, Çacatepec, Tlachquiauhco, Iolloxonecuillan, Atepec, Mictlan Tlauapan,[4] Nopalan, Iztac tlalocan, Cuextlan, Quetzaltepec, and Chichiualtatacalan.

In the days of this same [ruler] it befell that, eight years before the Spaniards came to arrive, it was seen, and taken as an omen, that by night a very great brilliance arose, like a flame. All night it stood shining. It appeared at the place where the sun came

caxtolxiuitl ipan nauhxiuitl, ipan muchiuh maianaliztli oxiujtl in manca in aocmo qujauja, ic noujian tepan cenman in mexicatl cenca netolinjloc in maianaliztica.

Çã no iehoatl ipan muchiuh, in oncan cujcacali catca in tenochtitlan, cuicac ce nepantla tecoc in tlaelnapaloa, queuh veiah noqueztepole uel xomjtotia, atlã tiuetztoçe. In muchiuh, y, ie iuh oalmachizti in Españoles.

Çã no iehoatl ipan mochiuh cioacoatl chocatinenca ioaltica, mochi tlacatl qujcaquja in chocaia qujtoaia. Nonopilhoantzitzi ic çan ie namechnocaujlia.

Çan no iehoatl ipan mochiuh. Çe tlacatl çihoatl ichan tenochtitlan mjc ica cocoliztli, njman motocac yitoalco ipan qujtemanque, ie iuh nauilhuitl motocac in cihoatl micquj mozcali ioaltica, cenca tlamauhti in vncan motocaca tlatatacco motlapo, auh in tetl ic motemanca vêca veuetzito: auh in iehoatl cihoatl in oiuh mozcali, njman qujnonotzato, qujlhujto in motecuçuma in tlein qujttac qujpouili, qujlhuj. Ca inic onjnozcali njmjtzilhujco. Ca ie ixqujch ca tehoatl moca tzonqujça in tlatocaiotl in mexico ca tehoatl mopan mantiaz in altepetl mexico. Aqujque in ie uitze ca iehoantin tlalmaceoaqujuj, iehoantin onozque in mexico: auh in iehoatl mjcca çihoatl ie no cempoalxiujtl oçe inen ioan oc ce qujchiuh iconeuh oquichtli:

Ioan miiec in altepetl qujpeuh motecuçuma in jtoca, icpatepec, cuezcomaixtlaoacan, çocollan, tecomaixtlaoacã, çacatepec, tlachqujauhco, iolloxonecuillan, atepec, mjctlan, tloapan, nopalan iztec tlalocan, cuextlan, quetzaltepec, chichioaltatacalan.

Çan no iehoatl ipan muchiuh, oc iuh chicuexiujtl aciqujui españoles mottaia netetzahujloa, in ioaltica oalmoquetzaia cenca tomaoac in tlanextli iuhqujn tlemjiaoatl iceoal tlanextiticaca tonatiuh iquiçaiampa oalmoquetzaia vmpoliuja in ie oalqujça tonatiuh,

2. The corresponding Spanish text mentions three years of famine.
3. *Cuicac ce nepantla tecoc.* The *Real Academia de la Historia MS* has *vei pantli. Nepantla* is clearly an error.
4. *Tlauapan.* Cf. corresponding Spanish text.

forth, and vanished when the sun was about to rise. For four years this always was to be seen at night. And when it disappeared, it was still four years before the Spaniards came to arrive.

And it came to pass that in his time the Spaniards came to arrive—they took and vanquished [the city of] Mexico here where the Spaniards now are, as well as all about here in New Spain. [This conquest was] in 1519.

The tenth ruler of Tenochtitlan.

Cuitlauac was the tenth, and he ruled eighty days after the Spaniards reached Mexico. In the time of this one, it happened that a great plague came, and that many died of it everywhere in the cities. It was said that it was the smallpox, the great raising of blisters. Never once had this been seen; never had it been suffered in Mexico. Indeed, it smote the faces of everyone, so that pits and roughnesses were formed. No longer were the dead buried; they could only cast them all into the water[5]—for in those times there was much water everywhere in Mexico. And there was a great, foul odor; the smell issued forth from the dead.

The eleventh ruler of Tenochtitlan.

Quauhtemoc was the eleventh, and he ruled Tenochtitlan four years. It came to pass in his reign that these Spaniards conquered and took the city of Mexico; and all the cities which lay surrounding. When he ruled, twelve priests, sons of Saint Francis, came and proceeded to reach [here]. They came to free men from idolatry and to teach the Faith.

The twelfth ruler of Tenochtitlan.

Don Andrés Motelchiuh was twelfth, and he ruled Tenochtitlan three years in the time of[6] the Spaniards, who went forth everywhere to conquests—to Cuextlan, to Honduras. And Nuño de Guzmán took him [in conquest] to Colhuacan, where he met his death.

The thirteenth ruler of Tenochtitlan.

Don Pablo Xochiquen was thirteenth, and he ruled Tenochtitlan three years.

nauhxiujtl in mochipa mottaia ioaltica auh in jcoac poliuh oc iuh nauhxiujtl açiqujui in españoles

ioan ipan mochiuh injc ipan açico españoles injc caçique injc qujpeuhque Mexico in vncan axcan onoque Españoles ioan in noujian in nican iancujc españa de mjll e qujnjentos y dezinueue.

Injc matlactli tenochtitlan tlatoanj.

Cujtlaoa, ic matlactli, tlatocat in tenochtitlan: nappoalilhujtl oiuh açico in Españoles mexico. Iehuatl ipan muchiuh in oalla vei cocoliztli, i cenca ic mjcoac in noujian altepetl ipan: mjto ca vej çaoatl, vej totomonaliztli: in aic ceppa omottac inin aic onecocoloc in mexico, vel mochi tlacatl, quĵtlacalhui in jxaiac: injc qujquiztic, chachaquachtic muchiuh, aocmo motocaia in mjmjcque, ça muchi atlan qujmontlaçaia: ca in jcoac cenca noujian atlan catca in mexico, ioã cenca tlaiaxtimomã, injc hijaxque mjmjcque.

Injc matlactli oce, tenochtitlan tlatoanj.

Quauhtemoc, ic matlactli oce tlatocat in tenochtitlan: nauhxiujtl, ipan muchiuh: injc iehoantin españoles qujpeuhque, caçique in altepetl in mexico, ioã in noujian ic qujiaoalotoc ixquich altepetl. Icoac tlâtocati in oallaque, açico matlactin omomen teupixque in ipilhoan Sanct frãcisco, in qujtecaoaltico tlateotoquiliztli: ioan qujtemachtique tlaneltoqujliztli.

Injc matlactlomome, tenochtitlan tlatoanj.

Don Andres, motelchiuh ic matlactli omome tlatocat in tenochtitlan exiujtl iepan españoles noujian iauqujçato in cuextlan, huduras, auh in iehoatl nonum de guzman, qujuicac in vej culhoacan vmpa mjqujto.

Injc matlactli omej, tenochtitlan tlatoanj.

Don pablo, xochiquen ic matlactli omej tlatocat in tenochtitlan: exiujtl.

---

5. *Ça muchi atlan.* The *Real Academia de la Historia MS* has *ca* for *ça.*
6. *Iepan: ye impan* in *ibid.*

4

The fourteenth ruler of Tenochtitlan.

Don Diego Vanitl was fourteenth, and he ruled Tenochtitlan four years.

The fifteenth ruler of Tenochtitlan.

Don Diego Teuetzquiti was fifteenth, and he ruled Tenochtitlan for thirteen years. It came to pass in his time that a great sickness came to be prevalent, known as a plague. From people's noses, blood issued; there was much death everywhere because of it, and there was death from famine. Very many were buried every day, everywhere. And in his time it was that the Chichimeca—those of Xochipilla—and the people of Cíbola were destroyed and conquered.

The sixteenth ruler of Tenochtitlan.

Don Cristóbal Cecepatic was sixteenth, and he ruled Tenochtitlan four years.

Injc matlactli onnauj tenochtitlan tlatoanj.

Don Diego vanjtl, ic matlactli onnauj tlatocat in tenochtitlan: nauhxiujtl.

Injc castolli tenochtitlan tlatoanj.

Don Diego teuetzqujti, ic castolli tlatocat in tenochtitlan: matlacxiujtl ipan exiujtl, ipan mochiuh inic momanaco vei cocoliztli mjtoa pestilencia teiacacpa quiz eztli cenca ic mjcoac in noujian ioan apizmjcoac cenca mjec in motocaia cemjlhujtl in noujiã. ioan ipan muchiuh injc poliuhque, peoaloque chichimeca, xochipilteca ioan Scipola tlaca.

Injc caxtolli oce, tenochtitlan tlatoanj.

Don xp̄oual cecepatic, ic caxtolli oce, tlatocat in tenochtitlan: nauhxiujtl.

Second Chapter, which telleth of the rulers who governed in Tlatilulco when the reign had not yet perished and when, later, once again the Spaniards gave back and restored [it] to them, until the year 1560.

The first ruler of Tlatilulco, Quaquapitzauac, who first began [the reign], governed Tlatilulco for sixty-two years. He conquered the people of Tenayuca, and Coacalco, and Xaltocan. When this one then ruled, two rulers of Tenochtitlan came together [one after the other], who were named Acamapichtli and Uitziliuitl.

The second ruler of Tlatilulco.
Tlacateotl [was] the second, and ruled Tlatilulco for thirty-eight years. It came to pass in his time that all the people of Acolhuacan and those of Coyoacan were conquered.

The third ruler of Tlatilulco.
Quauhtlatoa [was] the third, and ruled Tlatilulco for thirty-eight years. Two rulers, also, came together [one after the other], in Tenochtitlan. These [were] Itzcoatl and Moctezuma the Elder. It came to pass in his reign that the people of Azcapotzalco, and Coaixtlauacan, and Cuetlaxtlan, and Quauhtlinchan, and Xochimilco and all the people of Quauhnauac were destroyed and conquered.

The Fourth ruler of Tlatilulco.
Moquiuixtli [was] the fourth, and ruled Tlatilulco nine years. In his time the reign of Tlatilulco came to an end; for he and his brother-in-law, Axayacatl, ruler of Tenochtitlan, quarreled. [The latter] then made war upon Moquiuixtli and the people of Tlatilulco. And this Moquiuixtli of his own will quickly ascended to the summit of a [pyramid] temple, that he might cast himself from there; wherefore he then died.

Don Pedro Temilo: when he was made ruler of Tlatilulco, he was the one who again started the

Injc vme capitulo itechpa tlatoa in tlatoque in otlatocatque tlatilulco, in aiamo poliuj tlatocaiotl, ioan in çatepan oc ceppa oqujnmacaque oqujncuepilique españoles in ixqujchica ipan xiujtl de 1560.

Injc ce tlatilulco tlatoanj Quaquappitzaoac achto compeoalti tlatocat in tlatilulco iepoalxiujtl omome, qujmpeuh in tenaiocan tlaca, ioan coacalco ioan xaltocan, in iehoatl, y, ic tlatocat qujnnamjcticatca vmentin tlatoque in tenochtitlan in omoteneuhque Acamapichtli ioan vitziliujtl.

Injc vme tlatilulco tlatoanj.
Tlacateutl ic vme, tlatocat in tlatilulco, cempoalxiujtl ipan caxtolxiujtl omej, ipan muchiuh injc peoaloc ixqujch aculhoacatl ioan coioacatl.

Injc ei tlatilulco tlatoanj.
Quauhtlatoa, ic ei tlatocat in tlatilulco cempoalxiujtl ipan caxtolli omej xiujtl, qujnnamjcticatca no vmentin tlatoque catca in tenochtitlan, iehoatl itzcoatl, ioã veue motecuçuma. Ipan muchiuh injc poliuh injc peoaloc, azcaputzalcatl ioan coaixtlaoacã, ioã cuetlaxtlan, ioan quauhtlinchan, ioan xochmjlco ioan in jxqujch quauhnaoacatl.

Injc nauj tlatilulco tlatoanj.
Moqujujxtli, ic nauj tlatocat in tlatilulco: chicunauhxiujtl, ipã impoliuh tlatocaiotl tlatilulco, inic çan mococolique in jtex axaiaca tlatoanj tenochtitlan, injc qujiauchiuh moqujujxtli ioan tlatilulca. Auh in iehoatl moquiujxtli çan jnoma in tlecotiuetz iicpac teucalli injc vmpa oalmomaiauh injc vncan mjc.

Don pedro temjlo icoac omotlatocatlali in tlatilulco, iehoatl ie no compeoalti in tlatocaiotl, in oiuh

reign, when the Spaniards took and conquered the City of Mexico. The Spaniards, who had come from afar, went taking him with them everywhere when they conquered Cuextlan, Honduras, and Guatemala.

Don Martín Ecatl [was] the second who governed Tlatilulco. He ruled three years in the time of the Spaniards. In his time, it came to pass that [the demon] Ciuacoatl ate a small boy [as] he lay in his cradle there in Azcapotzalco. And in his time it happened that two eagles were[1] in separate wooden cages there in Tlatilulco. When for eight years they had been in wooden cages, eggs were laid; each eagle laid two eagle eggs.

Don Juan Auelittoc [was] the third, and he ruled Tlatilulco four years.

Don Juan Quauic onoc [was] the fourth, and ruled Tlatilulco seven years. And at the same time Don Pablo Xochiquen ruled Tenochtitlan. There came to pass in Tlatilulco a great marvel, a great example, [showing] how the world was to come to an end.

Don Alonso Quauhnochtli [was] the fifth, and he ruled Tlatilulco two years.

Don Martín Tlacatecatl [was] sixth, and he ruled Tlatilulco for six years. In his time there came to pass the aforementioned great plague and a war in which were conquered the Chichimeca—people of Nochtlan,[2]—and Cíbola, in the time of Don Antonio de Mendoza, Viceroy here in New Spain.

Don Diego Uitznauatlailotlac [was] the seventh to rule in Tlatilulco. In his time there was a great plague, known as the swellings of the neck, and many were the deaths from it. And this one ruled ten years.

conaçique compeuhque Españoles in altepetl mexico, noujian qujuicatinen in vêca españoles injc tepeuhque in cuextlan, hunduras, quauhtemallan.

Don Martin ,hêca ic vme tlatocat in tlatilulco: exiujtl ie impan in españoles. Ipan muchiuh, i çioacoatl qujqua piltzintli coçolco onoca vmpa azcaputzalco: ioan ipan muchiuh, vnteme quaquauhti quauhcalco manca no manca in vncã tlatilulco ic iuh chicuexiuitl mani quauhcalco motetique tlatlazque, oontetl in quauhtetl qujtlazque icecentetl quauhtli.

Don Iuan avellittoc ic ei tlatocat, in tlatilulco nauhxiujtl.

Don Iuan quaujc onoc, ic nauj tlatocat in tlatilulco chicoxiujtl ioan icoac tlatocati Don pablo xochiquen in tenochtitlã, in muchiuh tlatilulco vej tlamaujçolli vej neixcujtilli injc tlamjz cemanaoac

Don Alonso quauhnochtlj, ic macujlli tlatocat in tlatilulco oxjujtl.

Don Martin tlacateccatl, ic chiquacen tlatocat in tlatilulco chicoacexiujtl. Ipan muchiuh in omoteneuh vej cocoliztli ioan in iaoiutl injc peoaloque chichimeca, nochtlan tlaca, Scibola, ipan Don Antonjo de mendoça visorrej in njcan iancujc españa

Don diego vitznaoatlailotlac ic chicome tlatocat in tlatilulco. Ipan muchiuh vej cocoliztli, itoca quechpoçaoaliztli cenca ic mjcoac, auh in iehoatl matlacxiujtl in tlatocat.

---

1. For *manca no manca*, the *Real Academia de la Historia MS* has *manca no nonqua*.
2. In *ibid.*, *xochipilteca, yoan tototlan tlaca, yoan* follows *nochtlan tlaca*.

Third Chapter, where are told the rulers of Texcoco, and as many years as they governed.

The first ruler, who began the reign in Texcoco, was Tlaltecatzin. He ruled only eighty days, and nothing [of note] happened in his time. This one [was one of] the Chichimeca rulers.

And the second who became ruler, who followed Tlaltecatzin, was Techotlalatzin the Chichimeca. And he ruled seventy years; nor did anything [of note] occur in his time.

And the third who became ruler of Acolhuacan[1] was Ixtlilxochitl the Elder. He ruled for sixty-five years. [And] nothing [of note] befell in his time.

And the fourth who became ruler of Texcoco was Neçaualcoyotzin. He ruled seventy-one years. And at this time, in the time of Neçaualcoyotzin, the war was begun. The two, [Neçaualcoyotzin and] the ruler of Tenochtitlan, Itzcoatzin, conquered the Tepaneca, and they conquered people everywhere. Thereafter this Neçaualcoyotzin founded and laid down the seat of authority[2] of Acolhuacan or Texcoco.

And the fifth who became ruler of Texcoco was Neçaualpilli, and he ruled for fifty-three years. In his time war was made in all parts through which people were conquered. And when these two, Neçaualcoyotzin and Neçaualpilli, ruled, they were besieged by Tlaxcala and Uexotzinco.

And in the time of Neçaualpilli began what kept appearing, in the heavens, like a light, like a flame of

---

Injc ej capitulo vncan mjtoa in tezcuco tlatoque, injc izqui xiuitl tlatocatque.

Injc ce tezcuco tlatoanj, Qujpeoalti in tlatocaiutl in tezcuco iehoatl in tlaltecatzin çan napoalilhujtl in tlatocat atle ipan muchiuh, chichimeca tlatoque, y.

Auh injc vme tlatoanj muchiuh, in qujoaltoqujli in tlaltecatzin iehoatl in techotlalatzin chichimecatl, auh in tlatocat iepoalxiujtl ioan matlacxiujtl ano tle ipan muchiuh.

Auh injc ej, tlatoanj muchiuh acolhoacan iehoatl in veue ixtlilxochitl in tlatocat epoalxiujtl ioan macujlxiujtl amo tle ipan muchiuh.

Auh injc nauj tlatoanj muchiuh tezcuco iehoatl in neçaoalcoiotzin in tlatocat iepoalxiujtl ioan matlacxiujtl ioan cexiujtl, auh in iehoatl, y, in neçaoalcoiotzin ipan peuh in iaoiutl im omextin in tenochtitlan tlatoanj. Itzcoatzin inic qujpeuhque tepaneca: auh in noujian tepeuhque qujn iehoatl qujpeoalti in neçaoalcoiotzin in qujtecac in petlatl in jcpalli in acolhoacan tezcuco.

Auh injc macujlli, muchiuh tlatoanj tetzcuco, iehoatl in neçaoalpilli auh in tlatocat vmpoalxiujtl vn matlactli ioã exiujtl in jpan muchiuh iauiutl in noujian ic tepeoaloia auh in iehoantin im omextin in neçaoalcoiotzin ioan neçaoalpilli in jcoac tlatocatque tzacuticatca in tlaxcalla ioan vexotzinco.

Auh in neçaoalpilli ipan peuh in tlein oalmoquequetzaia ilhujcatitech in iuhquj tlanextlj in iuhquj

---

1. The corresponding Spanish text reads: *"señor de Tezcuco, o de Aculhoacan"*; cf. also Charles E. Dibble: *Códice Xolotl* (México: Universidades de Utah y de México, 1951), Pls. IIff. The term Acolhua refers to a grouping held together by kinship and political alliance occupying territory east of Lake Texcoco, with Texcoco as its center. Their main competitors for dominance in the valley were the Tepaneca, centered at Atzcapotzalco. On the Acolhua, see Fernando de Alva Ixtlilxóchitl: *Historia Chichimeca* (Mexico, 1892), pp. 41, 42, 49; also *Relaciones* (Mexico, 1891), p. 303. *"Y así juntó las ciudades y pueblos que eran de su parte de los aculhuas, que son Texcuco, Huexutla, Cohuatlichan." "Cohuatlichan de los aculhuas"* is referred to in *ibid.*, p. 293; *"Al último de estos tres, que era Tzontecoma, mancebo de poca edad, Señor de los aculhuas, le dió á Cohuatlichan con otros muchos pueblos y lugares donde los suyos poblasen como los demás sus compañeros"* (*ibid.*, p. 269).

2. *In petlatl, in icpalli*—the reed mat and the seat. In the corresponding Spanish text, Sahagún uses the term *señorjo*. The expression is illustrated thus figuratively in Andrés de Olmos: *Grammaire de la langue nahuatl ou mexicaine* (Rémi Siméon, ed.; Paris: Imprimerie Nationale, 1875), pp. 218, 221.

fire. It glowed each night. And for four years this came to pass. In the year count Seven Flint Knife it came to appear for the first time, and its disappearance [was] in the year count Eleven Flint Knife. And thus it persisted for four years. In many places mountains and crags broke up. And that which continued to appear, ended four years before the Spaniards came to arrive. And when Neçaualpilli died, [the Spaniards] were not yet present.

And the sixth who became ruler of Texcoco was Cacamatzin, who ruled four years. It came to pass in his time that the men from Castile arrived here.

And the seventh who became ruler of Texcoco was Coanacochtzin, who ruled five years. It was in the time of both [Coanacochtzin and] Quauhtemoctzin, ruler of Tenochtitlan, that the Mexicans were conquered.

And the eighth who became ruler of Texcoco was Tecocoltzin, who ruled one year in the time of the men from Castile. Already at this time the Marquis was in Texcoco; here preparations for war were made by which he vanquished the Mexicans.

The ninth who became ruler of Texcoco was Ixtlilxochitzin, who ruled eight years. And when the Mexicans were conquered, [the Spaniards] went taking him with them. He stood by the Marquis. And [the Marquis] took him to Uei mollan.[3] It came to pass that in their time the city [of Texcoco] was completely quieted, that the Marquis and Coanacochtli together set [affairs] in order.

The tenth who became ruler of Texcoco [was] Yoyontzin. He governed one year.

The eleventh who became ruler of Texcoco [was] Tetlaueuetzquititzin. He governed five years.

The twelfth who became ruler of Texcoco [was] Don Antonio Tlauitoltzin. He governed six years.

The thirteenth who became ruler of Texcoco [is]

tlemjiaoatl iceioal tlanextitica, auh nauhxiujtl in jpan muchiuh ipan xiuhtonalli chicome tecpatl in iancujcan necico auh impoliuh ipan xiuhtonalli matlactloce tecpatl auh injc tlamanca nauhxiujtl mjieccan xiti tepetl in texcalli auh in jcoac poliuh in tlen oalmoquequetzaia oc iuh nauhxiujtl aciquiuj in *Españoles,* auh icoac mjc in neçaoalpilli aocmo ixpan

Auh injc chicoacen tlatoanj muchiuh tetzcuco iehoatl in cacamatzin in tlatocat nauhxiujtl. Iehoatl ipã muchiuh injc açico njcan castillan tlaca

Auh injc chicome tlatoanj muchiuh tetzcuco, iehoatl in Coanacochtzin in tlatocat macujlxiujtl iehoatl ipã muchiuh injc peoaloque mexica im omextin quauhtemoctzin tenochtitlan tlatoanj.

Auh injc chicuej tlatoanj muchiuh tetzcuco iehoatl in tecocoltzin in tlatocat cexiujtl ie imjxpan in Castillan tlaca ie icoac in tetzcuco catca marques vncan moiauchichiuh injc qujmpeuh mexica.

Injc chicunhauj tlatoanj muchiuh tetzcuco iehoatl in ixtlilxochitzin in tlatocat chicuexiujtl auh in icoac peoaloque mexica qujujcatiuja in marques itlan ommoquetz ioã qujuicaia in vej mollan iehoãtin imjxpan muchiuh injc vel motlatlali altepetl injc tlauellalali marques nehoan coanacuchtli.

Injc matlactlj tlatoanj muchiuh tetzcuco iehoatl in ioiontzin in tlatocat cexiujtl.

Injc matlactloçe tlatoanj muchiuh tetzcuco iehoatl in tetlaueuetzqujtitzin in tlatocat macujlxiujtl.

Injc matlactlomome tlatoanj muchiuh tetzcuco iehoatl in don Antonjo tlaujtoltzin in tlatocat chicoacexiujtl.

Injc matlactlj omej tlatoanj muchiuh tetzcuco,

3. Cf. *Codex of 1576* (J. M. Aubin: *Histoire de la nation mexicaine. . . . Réproduction du Codex de 1576* [Paris: Maísonneuve Frères, Editeurs, 1893]), p. 87, and *Mapa de Tepechpan.*

the present ruler, Don Hernando Pimentel, who hath governed nearly twenty years.[4]

And in all the time that the Acolhua kept the reign, in all, have been counted three hundred and four years until the time the Spaniards arrived.[5]

iehoatl in axcan tlatoanj don hernando pimentel in otlatocat achi cẽpoalxiujtl

Auh ie ixqujch caujtl qujpia in tlatocaiotl in aculhoaque in ie ic mocempoa caxtolpoalxiujtl ioan nauhxiujtl. in ixquich cauitl in oacico españoles

---

4. The *Real Academia de la Historia MS* (*Primeros memoriales*, Chap. III) has, for *achi cempoalxiuitl* (nearly twenty years), *ecastolxiuitl* (fifteen years).

5. In *ibid.*, this last paragraph reads, in part, varying from the *Florentine Codex*: "*y ye ic mocempoa castolpoalxiuitl yoan napoalxiuitl yoan nauhxiuitl yn ixquichica axcã ipan ticate xiuhtonalli vmacatl*" (384 years until the year sign Two Reed in which we now are).

Fourth Chapter, in which are recorded the rulers of Uexotla.

Behold, the Chichimeca rulers of Uexotla were known as Acolhua. There the Acolhua Chichimeca first arrived.

The first who became ruler of Uexotla [was] Maçatzin tecutli. He ruled seventy-eight years.

The second ruler [was] Tochin tecutli. He ruled thirty-eight years.

The third ruler [was] Ayotzin tecutli. He ruled seventy-four years.

The fourth ruler [was] Quatlauice tecutli. He ruled fifty-five years.

The fifth ruler was named Totomochtzin; he ruled fifty-two years. And these five Chichimeca rulers, who maintained well the government [of Uexotla], exacted tribute from no one in the three hundred[1] years in which they [thus] maintained well their sovereignty.

The sixth ruler was named Iaotzin tecutli; he ruled fifty-eight years.[2] In his time the Acolhua Chichimeca began to exact tribute of [those of] Tepanoayan.

The seventh ruler was named Xilotzin tecutli. He ruled twenty-eight years.

The eighth ruler was named Itlacauhtzin. He ruled twenty-eight years.

The ninth ruler was named Tlaçolyaotzin; he ruled fifty-eight years.[3] At about this time it came

Injc nahuj capitulo vncan motenehoa in tlatoque vexutla.

Izcate in chichimeca tlatoque catca vexutla in moteneoa aculoaque in vmpa achto açico aculhoacan chichimeca.

Injc ce tlatoanj muchiuh uexutla Maçatzin tecutli in tlatocat epoalxiujtl ipan caxtolxiujtl ioan exiujtl.

Injc vme tlatoanj tochin tecutli in tlatocat cempoalxiujtl ipan caxtolxiujtl ioan exiujtl.

Injc ei tlatoanj aiotzin tecutli in tlatocat epoalxiujtl ipã matlacxiujtl ioan nauhxiujtl.

Injc nahuj tlatoanj quatlauiçe tecutli in tlatocat vmpoalxiujtl ioan caxtolxiujtl.

Injc macujlli tlatoanj itoca totomochtzin in tlatocat vmpoalxiujtl ipan matlacxiujtl ioan vnxiujtl auh in jmacujlixtin, y, chichimeca tlatoque in uel qujpiaia in jtlatocaio in acampa tequjtia caxtolpoalxiujtl in uel qujpix in jtlatocaio.

Injc chiquacen tlatoanj itoca iautzin tecutli in tlatocat vmpoalxiujtl ioan caxtolxiujtl ipan exiujtl iehoatl ipan peuh injc tequjtque tepanoaia chichimeca aculhoaque.

Injc chicome tlatoanj itoca xilotzin tecutli in tlatocat cempoalxiujtl ipan chicuexiujtl.

Injc chicuej tlatoanj itoca itlacauhtzin in tlatocat cempoalxiujtl ipan chicuexiujtl.

Injc chicunauj tlatoanj itoca tlaçoliautzin in tlatocat vmpoalxiujtl ioan caxtolxiujtl ioan exiujtl quj

---

1. In the *Real Academia de la Historia MS* (*Primeros memoriales,* Chap. III), the Nahuatl text reads *castolpoalxiuitl ioan matlacxiuitl ioan exiuitl* (313 years).
2. Corresponding Spanish text reads 53 years.
3. Corresponding Spanish text reads 53 years.

to pass that the seat of authority was established in Texcoco, so that Neçaualcoyotzin was invested with rule. [Their periods of rule] came together—[that of] Tlaçolyaotzin of Uexotla [and that of Neçaualcoyotzin].

The tenth ruler was named Tzontemoctzin. He ruled fifteen years.

The eleventh ruler was named Cuitlauatzin. He ruled forty-one years.

The twelfth ruler was named Tzapocuetzin. He ruled thirteen years.

The thirteenth ruler was likewise called Cuitlauatzin; only he succeeded [the former]. He ruled thirteen years.

And all the time [until] now, up to the year we are in—when the government was held in Uexotla—thus is added up to five hundred and sixty-two years, until the present year-sign, Two Reed.

iehoatl ipan muchiuh injc motecac petlatl icpalli tetzcuco injc motecutlali neçaoalcoiotzin monamicque tlaçoliautzin vexutla.

Injc matlactli tlatoanj, itoca tzontemoctzin: in tlatocat caxtolxiujtl.

Injc matlactloce tlatoanj, itoca Cuitlaoatzin: in tlatocat vmpoalxiujtl ioan cexiujtl.

Injc matlactlomome tlatoanj, itoca tzapocuetzin: in tlatocat matlacxiujtl ioan exiujtl.

Injc matlactli omej tlatoanj, çan no itoca Cujtlaoatzin, çã tetoca: in tlatocat matlacxiujtl ioan exiujtl.

Auh in ie ixquich caujtl, ascan ipan in xiujtl ticate: in ie ic mocempoa, in mopia tlatocaiotl vexutla: ie centzonxiujtl, ioan chicuepoalxiujtl ioan oxiujtl, in ixqujchica ipan axcan xiuhtonalli, vmacatl.

Fifth Chapter, in which it is told how many four hundreds of years ago Tollan was destroyed, up to [the present] year of 1565.

The city of Tollan [was] a very large city, and truly a marvel. A great many powerful and wise men lived there. Their history will be told in the Tenth Book. And how they were destroyed, how they dispersed and people fled—all [this] will be related there. But in this chapter, all that is to be said is how many four hundreds of years [it hath been] since the Toltecs were destroyed.

This was in [the year] one thousand, one hundred and ten; from there [the count] reacheth and endeth at this year, 1565.[1] And twenty-two years after Tollan was destroyed, the Chichimeca came to reach and take the land and establish themselves there in Texcoco.

And the first who became their leader, something like their ruler, became so in the year of the birth of Our Lord Jesus Christ, 1246. And the [first] ruler of Azcapotzalco, who was named Teçoçomoctli, [became so] in the year of the birth of Our Lord Jesus Christ, 1348. And the [first] ruler of Mexico, Acamapichtli, [became so] in [the year] of the birth [of Our Lord], 1384. And the ruler of Tlacopan, whose name was Chimalpopoca, died[2] in the year of Our Lord Jesus Christ, 1489.

Injc macujlli capitulo, ipan mjtoa: in ie quezqujtzonxiujtl poliuh tullan, in jxquichica xiujtl, de 1565.

In altepetl tullan, cenca vej altepetl, uel maujztic: cenca mjiequjntin vncan nenca, in chicaoaque, in tlamatinj in jntlatollo mjtoz in jpan ic matlactli amoxtli. Ioan in quen opoliuh, in quenjn oxixitin, omomoiaoac: muchi oncan mjtoz. Auh in jpan, y, capitulo çan ie ixqujch vncan mjtoa, in ie quezqujtzonxiujtl, in opoliuhque tulteca.

Ca ie ontzonxiujtl ipan caxtolpoalxiujtl, ipan matlacxiujtl: oncan oallaci, oncan oallamj injn xiujtl, 1565. Auh ie iuh, cempoalxiujtl omome, opoliuh in tullan: in açico in tlalmaçeoaco: omotecaco in chichimeca, in vncan tetzcuco.

Auh in iancujcan inteiacancauh muchiuh, in iuhqujma intlatocauh muchiuh ipan in tlacat in jxiuhtzin in totecujo iesu xp̄o. 1246. Auh in azcaputzalco tlatoanj in moteneoa teçoçomoctli ipan in tlacat in jxiuhtzin totecujo Iesu xp̄o. 1348. Auh in mexico tlatoanj, in acamapichtli ipan in tlacat, 1384. Auh in tlacopã tlatoanj, catca in jtoca chimalpopoca, ipan in mic ixiuhtzin totecujo Iesu xp̄o. 1489.

1. Corresponding Spanish text reads 1571.
2. *Mic:* in the MS, this could be read either *mic* or *inic*.

Sixth Chapter, in which it is told how signs and omens appeared and were seen, when the Spaniards had not yet come to this land, and when they were yet unknown to the dwellers here.

When the Spaniards were not to arrive here for ten years, an omen first appeared in the heavens like a flame, a tongue of fire, as if it were showering the light of the dawn.[1] It appeared as if it were piercing the heavens; it was wide at the base and pointed at the top. Well into the midst of the heavens, well into their center it stood reaching; well into the heart of the heavens it was arriving. [That which] thus was seen arose there to the east,[2] and when midnight had passed, it appeared that dawn was breaking. When day broke, soon the sun destroyed it when he arose. For a whole year it came forth (it was in [the year sign] Twelve House that it began), and when it appeared, there was much crying out as they struck their mouths with their hands. All were frightened; all waited in dread.

The second omen came to pass here in Mexico. Of its own accord, fire broke out and burned fiercely in the house of the devil Uitzilopochtli. No one set fire to it; of its own accord it took fire. It is said that the name of the place[3] was Tlacateccan. When [the fire] appeared, already the squared, wooden pillars were blazing. From within, the flame, the tongues and flames of fire, came forth. Very quickly it consumed all the house beams. Then there was shouting; [the priests] said: "Mexicans! Run here to extinguish [the fire! Bring] your earthen water jars!" And when they poured water upon it, when they tried to put it out, still more did it flare up. It could not be extinguished, and it burned completely.

[As] the third omen, a temple was struck by a thunder bolt.[4] It was only a straw hut, a place named

Ic chiquacen capitulo, vncan mjtoa in nez, in mottac, in machiotl, ioan in tetzaujtl, in aiamo oalhuj españoles in njcan tlalli ipan, ioan in aiamo iximachoia, in njcan chaneque.

In aiamo oallaci españoles, oc matlacxiujtl: centlamantli tetzaujtl achto nez ilhujcatitech, iuhquj in tlemjiaoatl, iuhqujn tlecueçallotl, iuhqujn tlaujzcalli pipixauhticaca, injc neçia iuhqujn ilhujcatl qujçoticac, tzimpatlaoac, quapitzaoac, uel inepantla in jlhujcatl, uel iiolloco in açiticac ilhujcatl, vel ilhujcaiollotitech açiticac in iuh ittoia vmpa tlapcopa in oalmoquetzaia, oiuh onqujz ioalnepantla in neçia tlathujliaia, ipan tlathuja. Qujn iehoatl qujoalpoloaia in tonatiuh, in jcoac oalqujçaia: uel cexiujtl in oalmoquetzaia (ipan matlactlomome calli in peuh) auh in jcoac neçia tlacaoacaia, netenujtecoia, neiçaujloia, tlatemmachoia.

Injc vntetl tetzaujtl muchiuh, njcan mexico, çan monomauj in tlatlac cuetlan, aiac ma qujtlecauj çan monoma tlecauj, in jcal diablo vitzilobuchtli mjtoaia itocaiocan tlacatecca in nez ie tlatla in tlaquetzalli iitic oalqujça in tlemjiaoatl, in tlenenepilli, in tlecueçallutl, cenca çan iciuhca compalo in ixqujch calquaujtl. Niman ie ic tlacaoaca qujtoa. Mexicae, ma oallatotoca, tla ceujloz, amapilol: auh in jcoac caatequiaia, in qujceujznequja, çan ie ilhujce mopitza aocmo uel çeuh uellallac.

Injc etetl tetzaujtl, vitecoc ipan tlatlatzin teucalli, çan xacalli catca, itocaiocan tzommolco, iteupan in

1. This may be clarified by reference to Pl. 4, Book XII.

2. Cf. variant versions in Chaps. I and III, and in Book XII, Chap. I, as well as in the Nahuatl version in the *Real Palacio MS,* the corresponding Spanish text, and Eduard Seler: *Einige Kapitel aus dem Geschichtswerk des Fray Bernardino de Sahagun aus dem Aztekischen übersetzt* (Caecilie Seler-Sachs, Walter Lehmann, Walter Krickeberg, eds.; Stuttgart: Strecker und Schroeder, 1927), p. 453. Alternative translations appear to be possible.

3. *Mjtoaia itocaiocan:* in a similar passage, the *Memoriales en 3 Columnas* (Francisco del Paso y Troncoso: *Fr. Bernardino de Sahagún—Historia de las Cosas de Nueva España* [Madrid: Hauser y Menet, 1906], VII, p. 93) has *mitoaya, ytepeyoc, ytocayocā.* Cf. also Pl. 5, Book XII.

4. Cf. Pl. 6 ,Book XII.

Tzonmulco, the Temple of Xiuhtecutli. It was not raining hard, but only sprinkling. This was taken as an omen of evil, [for] it was said that it was only a summer flash, and that thunder did not sound.

[As] the fourth sign of evil, [while] there was still sun, a comet fell. It became three parts and began from where the sun set and went toward where he arose. It went as if showering sparks; for a great distance its wake went extending; far out did its tail reach. And when it was seen, there was much shouting; like [the rattle of] shells[5] it spread about.

[As] the fifth omen, the water [of the lake] foamed up, and the wind did not stir it up. It was as if it welled up, as if it boiled up with a cracking noise. Very far did it go as it rose upward, and it reached the lower parts of the houses; and, wet by the water, the houses crumbled. This was the great lake which extendeth by us here in Mexico.[5a]

[As] the sixth omen, often was heard a woman, who went weeping and crying out at night. She cried out loudly; she went about saying: "O my beloved sons, now we are at the point of going!" Sometimes she said: "My beloved sons, whither shall I take you?"

[As] the seventh omen, at one time the fisher folk hunted or snared with nets. They took a bird of ashen hue, like a crane. Then they came to show it to Moctezuma, [who was in] the Tlillan calmecac.[6] The sun was past his zenith, and there was yet daylight. There was what was like a mirror upon its head—round, disc-like, and as if pierced. From it appeared the heavens—the fire drill, the stars. And Moctezuma took it as a most evil omen when he saw the stars and the fire drill. And when he gazed a second time at the bird's head, beyond, he beheld what appeared to be like a number of people, coming massed, coming as conquerors, coming in war panoply. Deer bore them upon their backs. And then he summoned the astrologers[7] and the wise men, and said to them: "Do you not know what I have

xiuhtecutli, amo tilaoaia, çan aoachqujauja in iuh tetzammachoc, iuh mjto in ca çã tonalhujtecoc, amono caquiztic in tlatlatzinjliztli.

Injc nauhtetl tetzamachiotl, oc vnca in tonatiuh in xiujtl vetz: ieteetia, vmpa oalpeuh in tonatiuh icalaqujampa, auh vmpa itztia in jqujçaiampa, iuhqujn tlexuchtli pipixauhtiuh, ueca mocujtlapiltitiuh, veca açitiuh in jcuitlapil. Auh in oittoc cenca tlacaoacac, iuhqujn oioalli onmoma.

Injc macujltetl tetzaujtl, poçon in atl amo i ehecatl qujpoçonalti, iuhquj mumuloca, iuhquj xixitemumoloca: cenca veca in ia injc macoquetz, auh in calli tzitzintla cacic auh capapachiuh xixitin in calli iehoatl in vej atl totlan manj njcan mexico.

Injc chiquacentlamantli tetzaujtl, mjiecpa çihoatl cacoia chocatiuh, tzatzitiuh, ioaltica, cenca tzatzi: qujtotinemj, nonopilhoantzitzin ie ic çan ie touj: in quenmanja qujtoa, nonopilhoantzitzin campa namechnoujqujliz.

Injc chicuntlamantli tetzaujtl, ceppa tlatlamaia, manoço tlamaitlaujaia in atlaca, centetl caçique tototl, nextic: iuhqujn tocujlcoiotl. Niman qujttilico in motecuçuma, tlillan calmecac omotzcalo in tonatiuh, oc tlaca: iuhqujn tezcatl icpac manj, malacachtic, teujlacachtic, iuhquj xapotticac: vnpa onneçia in ilhujcatl: inmamalhoaz in çiçitlalti. Auh in motecuçuma cenca qujmotetzauj in jcoac qujmjttac çiçitlalti ioan mamalhoaztli: auh injc oppa ontlachix, in jcpac tototl: ene qujttac iuhquj on in ma acame moquequetztitiujtze, tepeuhtiujtze moiauchichiuhtiuitze qujnmama mamaça, auh njman qujnnotz in tlaçiuhque in tlamatinjme qujmjlhuj. Amo anquimati, in tlein onoconjttac iuhqujn acame moquequetztiujtze. Auh ie qujnanqujlizquja in conjttaque opoliuh aoc tle uel qujtoque.

---

5. The term *oioalli* appears to be capable of interpretations as rattle, bell, or shell. Cf. Arthur J. O. Anderson and Charles E. Dibble: *Florentine Codex*, Book I, *The Gods* (Santa Fe: The School of American Research and The University of Utah, 1950), p. 1, and Book VII, *Sun, Moon, and Stars* (1953), Appendix, where, under *Tonatiuh qualo*, Sahagún's note 7 translates *oyoualli moteca*. Cf. also Eduard Seler: *Gesammelte Abhandlungen zur Amerikanischen Sprach- und Alterthumskunde* (Berlin: A. Asher & Co., 1904), II, pp. 428, 462.

Cf. also Zelia Nuttall: *The Book of the Life of the Ancient Mexicans* (Berkeley: University of California, 1903), Part I, fols. 8, 48, where the *oyoalli* are pictured in an anonymous Codex in Florence, Italy.

5a. After *cacic*, the *Memoriales en 3 Columnas* reads: "*Auh ceq' papachiuh cequi xixitin*"; after *manj*: "*Auh ynic mocuep ynic ceceuh çã no vmpa ya ỹ vmpa vatztia ỹ vey apãpa.*"

6. Corresponding Spanish text: "*en su palacio, en vna sala, que llamauan Tlillan calmecac.*" Cf. Fray Bernardino de Sahagún: *Historia general de las cosas de Nueva España* (México: Editorial Pedro Robredo, 1938), IV, pp. 24-25 (note c).

7. *Tlaçiuhque*: cf. Ángel María Garibay K: "Paralipómenos de Sahagún," *Tlalocan*, II, 2 (1946), pp. 167, 171.

After *opoliuh*, the *Memoriales en 3 Columnas* reads: "*aoc tle vel q'toqz. oc ceppa q'milhvi ỹ tlaciuhqz. yn tlamatinime, tle ynin tototl quilhviqz amo ne yehoatl in quatezcatl.*"

seen there, like a number of people coming massed?"
And when they were about to answer, that which
they looked at vanished. They could say nothing.

[As] eighth omen, often were discovered mis-
shapen people. They had two heads, but only one
body. They took them there to the Tlillan calmecac,
where Moctezuma beheld them. When he had
looked at them, then they vanished.

Injc chicuetetl tetzaujtl, mjiecpa motenextiliaia
tlaca, tlacanetzolti, ontetzontecomeque, ça ce in
jntlac vnpa qujmonujcaia in tlillan calmecac, vmpa
qujmjttaia in motecuçuma: in oqujttac njman
poliujia.

Seventh Chapter, in which are told many things which came to pass when the Spaniards had not yet come to this land, until the year '50.*

In the year 1519, when the Captain, Don Hernando Cortés, came to sally forth, very many boats came, in which the Spanish host traveled. And when Moctezuma knew of it, then he sent his emissaries, and they carried as greetings very many and costly articles.

And they thought that Quetzalcoatl had come. And when he went to arrive, then they gave and took all [which they carried] as greetings to this Captain, Don Hernando Cortés.

And when these Spaniards came to enter [the land], then the Tlaxcalans' Otomí[1] [warriors] went to meet them in battle. Not few, but very many thus fought and waged war with the Spaniards. And all of the Tlaxcalans' Otomí [warriors] died; the Spaniards slew them. By this were the Tlaxcalans much frightened, and these Tlaxcalans then sent messengers, [who] went to offer them food and all which they might need. And they welcomed them and escorted them to the homes of Tlaxcala.

And for a few days the Spaniards tarried and rested there. And the Spaniards then went there to Cholula. There they slew many Cholulans.

And after this, when Moctezuma had heard of it, he was much frightened; and all the people of Tenochtitlan were exceeding fearful. So once again he sent messengers. These whom this Moctezuma sent, lords and noblemen, went to meet the Captain, Don Hernando Cortés; they took with them a great deal of gold. And they went to meet him there between Popocatepetl and Iztac ciuatl, [at a place] named Itualco.[2] There they conferred [with Cortés; one of]

Injc chicome capitulo, vncan mjtoa mjiec tlamantli in inpan muchiuh in aiamo oalhuj españoles in njcan tlalli ipan, in jxqujchica vnpoalxiujtl ommatlactli.

In jpan xiujtl 1519 icoac qujçaco in capitan don hernando cortes, cenca mjiec in acalli oalla in vncan oalietiaque in españoles in iauqujzque: auh in oiuh qujma in iehoatl motecuçuma, njman tlaihoaiaque in jtitlanhoan, auh in qujtqujque in tetlapaloliztli cenca mjiec, ioan cenca tlaçotli in tlatqujtl.

Auh momatque, ca iehoatl in quetzalcoatl ohoalla: auh in jcoac oaçito njman mochi qujmamacaque in qujtqujque tetlapaloliztli, in iehoatl, capitan don hernando cortes.

Auh in jcoac ie calactiujtze, in iehoantin españoles: njman qujiaunamjqujto, in tlaxcalteca, imotonhoan: amo çan quexqujchtin, cenca mjiequjntin, ic oqujmjcalque, oqujniauchiuhque, in españoles. Auh mochintin, mjcque in tlaxcalteca imotonhoan, qujnmjctique, in españoles: ic cenca momauhtique, in tlaxcalteca, auh in iehoantin, in tlaxcalteca, njmã ic tlaihoaque, qujnmacato in tlaqualli, in jxqujch intech monequj: ioan qujnpaccatlapaloto: ioan qujnhujcaque, in vmpa inchan in tlaxcallan.

Auh çan quezqujlhujtl, in vncan motlalique, moçeujque, in iehoantin españoles. Auh in iehoantin, españoles njman iaque in vmpa chololan: vncan mjiequjntin, qujnmjctique, in chololteca.

Auh in jcoac, oiuh qujcac, in iehoatl motecuçuma, cenca momauhti: ioã yn jxqujchtin, in tenochca cenca momauhtique: ic oc ceppa tlaihoa, in iehoatl motecuçuma iehoantin in qujmjhoa in tetecuti, in pipiltin, qujnamjqujto, in capitan, don hernando cortes: cenca mjiec, in qujtqujque, in teucujtlatl. Auh vncan in qujnamjqujto, in jtzalan popoca tepetl: ioan in jztac tepetl, in moteneoa ithoalco. Vncan qujnonotzque, qujmacaque in jtlatol, in jta motecu-

---

* Corresponding Spanish text: *"hasta el año de 30."*

   1. Cf. Anderson and Dibble, *op. cit.,* II, p. 102; Seler, *Einige Kapitel,* p. 476, n. 1, citing Tezozomoc, cap. 66. Cf. also Sahagún (Robredo ed.), IV, pp. 43ff., 149-150, n. 1.

   See also Book XII, Chap. xi.

   2. Ithualco: in Rémi Siméon: *Dictionnaire de la langue nahuatl ou mexicaine* (Paris: Imprimerie Nationale, 1885), it is described as a *"Mont qui domine à l'orient la vallée de Mexico."*

Moctezuma's elder[s] delivered his message. And they offered him all [the gifts with which] they greeted him. They extended to him the gold and still other [goods].

And [the Spaniards] came straight here to Mexico. When Don Hernando Cortés came to arrive, he readied himself for war. And Moctezuma went to meet him there by the houses [of the outskirts of Mexico], there at Xolloco. He went to receive him in peace. And he offered him adoration and greeted the Captain, Don Hernando Cortés. Then he took him there to the great palace. There all the Spaniards remained.

And after some days, the Captain imprisoned Moctezuma.

And when word arrived from the coast that still more Spaniards had arrived, the Captain went to meet them; he took some Spaniards with him, and [some] natives. And he left here Don Pedro Alvarado and still other Spaniards to guard the palace.

And when came the feast day of Uitzilopochtli, Don Pedro Alvarado and the Spaniards who were with him slew many Mexicans while they were observing the feast day of Uitzilopochtli. Thus war began.

And when the Captain returned from the coast, he brought many Spaniards. Not on this account did the Mexicans defer; they spread the war considerably.

And the year 1520 was when Moctezuma died. And the Spaniards arose and went to Tlaxcala. And there befell a great plague here in Mexico; there was smallpox; and very many of the natives died.

In the year 1521, the Spaniards came once more. They stayed there in Texcoco. After some time they made war, and they vanquished and fought the Mexicans.

In the year 1522, once again the Mexicans gathered themselves and came together, those who had been dispersed and broken up because of the war.

And the year 1524 was when the twelve Franciscan Fathers arrived to convert the natives of New Spain.

çuma: ioan qujmacaque in jxqujch in jntetlapaloaia, injn tetech açia, in teucujtlatl, ioan oc cequj.

Auh çan oallamelauh, in njcan mexico, injc açico in iehoatl, don hernando cortes, çan oalmoiauchichiuhtia, auh in motecuçuma, vmpa in qujnamjqujto in caltenco, in vmpa xolloco, çan qujpaccanamjqujto: ioan qujtlatlauhti, qujtlapalo in capitan don hernando cortes, njman qujujcac in vmpa vej tecpan vncan motlalique, in jxqujchtin españoles.

Auh in jquezqujlhujioc, in iehoatl capitan oqujlpi in motecuçuma:
auh in jcoac oaçico tlatolli, in vmpa atenco: injc oc centlamantin oaçico españoles: in iehoatl capitan oqujnnamjqujto, cequjntin qujnujcac españoles, ioan njcan tlaca: auh njcan qujcauhtia in don pedro aluarado, ioan oc cequjntin españoles in tecpan tlapiaia.

Auh in jquac in oqujz ilhujuh vitzilobuchtli, in iehoatl don pº aluarado, ioan in espanoles in jtlan catca, mjiequjntin, qujnmjctique in mexica, in qujlhujqujxtiliaia vitzilobuchtli, ic vmpeuh in iauiotl.

Auh in jcoac in ooalmocuep, in capitan: in vmpa atenco, mjiequjntin, qujnoalhujcac españoles, amo ic motlacaoaltique in mexica, cenca qujtototzaia in iaujutl.

Auh in jpan xiujtl 1520 icoac omjc in motecuçuma, auh in iehoantin españoles, oqujzque tlaxcallan iaque: auh uej cocoliztli muchiuh in njcan mexico, çaçaoatioac: ioan cenca mjiequjntin mjcque, in njcan tlaca.

In jpan xiujtl 1521, oc ceppa oallaque in españoles, ompa omotlalique, in tetzcuco, uecauhtica qujniauchiuhque, qujmpeuhque, qujmjcalque, in mexica.

In jpan xiujtl 1522, oc ceppa oalmonechicoque, oalmocentlalique in mexica: in moiaoaca in xitinca in jpampa iauiutl

Auh in jpan xiujtl 1524, icoac açico in matlactin vmomen sãct francisco padreme, in qujntlaneltoqujtique in njcan nueua españa tlaca.

Eighth Chapter, in which are told the various articles with which they adorned the rulers and noblemen—which they placed on them when they were bedight in capes and breech clouts.

The cape with the serpent mask design, bordered with eyes;[1]

The cape with the conch shell design, bordered with eyes;[2]

The cape with a design of stone discs, bordered with eyes;[3]

The cape with the obsidian serpent design, bordered with eyes;[4]

The cape with wine-god jar design, bordered with eyes;[5]

The cape with the butterfly design, bordered with eyes;

The cape with an eagle's face painted on it, bordered with eyes;[6]

The red-bordered ocelot cape, in the middle of which stood an ocelot;[7]

The cape of dark green diagonally divided, in the middle of which stood an obsidian eagle;[8]

The cape of blue knots diagonally divided,[9] on which a spear-eagle stood;

The maguey fiber cape, with an ocelot tail pendant;

The cape of shining maguey fiber [ornamented with] flattened heads;

The orange cape with the wind jewel[10] [design] and the feathered border;

The orange cape with a striped border;

The light blue cape with a wind jewel design, which had a border of feathers with spirals;

The carmine-colored cape with an eye border;

Injc chicuei capitulo, vncan mjtoa in jzqujtlamantli: in nechichioaia tlatoque in pipilti in jntech qujtlaliaia, injc mocencaoaia in tilmatli in maxtlatl.

Coaxaiacaio tilmatli, tenjxio,

tecucizio tilmatli tenjxio,

temalacaio tilmatli tenjxio,

itzcoaio tilmatli tenjxio,

vmetochtecomaio tilmatli tenjxio,

papaloio tilmatli tenjxio,

xaoalquauhio tilmatli tenjxio,

ocelotentlapalli iitic icac oçelotl,

chicoiapalli nacazmjnquj iitic icac itzquauhtli,

xiuhtlalpilnacazmjnquj, tlacochquauhtli vncan icac,

quetzalichtilmatli ocelocujtlapillo

quetzalichpetztli, quapatlacio tilmatli,

camopalecacozcaio, tenjujio tilmatli,

camopaltenoaoanquj tilmatli,

apalecacozcaio tilmatli, iujtica tentlaiaoalo,

nochpaltilmatli tenjxio,

---

1. Fol. 16r of Book VIII of the *Florentine Codex* defines the border with eyes or eyelets. Also see corresponding Spanish text.
2. Cf. James Cooper Clark: *Codex Mendoza* (London: Waterlow and Sons, 1938), III, fol. 46.
3. Cf. corresponding Spanish text.
4. Cf. Clark, *op. cit.,* fol. 31.
5. Cf. *loc. cit.*
6. Cf. *ibid.,* fol. 49. An alternative translation might be "the colored eagle feather cape."
7. Cf. *ibid.,* fol. 31. See also Seler, *Gesammelte Abhandlungen,* II, p. 522.
8. *Itzquauhtli*: see, however, Sahagún, *op. cit.,* III, p. 181.
9. *Xiuhtlalpilli* might refer to a design suggested by the ceremony of tying the years.
10. See, however, corresponding Spanish text, in which *ecacozcatl* is described as a flower; see also Book VIII of the Codex, fol. 16v.

The tawny cape with a spiral border;

The coyote fur cape with a spiral border;

The tawny, knotted cape;

The cape with scorpion design stripes;

The tawny cape with the water spider;

The tawny cape with the butterfly;

The ocelot cape;

The cape with the eagle's leg;

The cape with the ocelot skin step design;[11]

The ocelot cape;

The half-ocelot, half-eagle cape;

The tawny cape provided with the design of an eye upon a hooked element;[12]

The cape with the design of a ladder on the earth;

The cape with an embroidered, radiating design;

The cape of duck feathers with a colored border;

The cape of duck feathers with [a design of] flattened heads;

The white duck feather cape, bordered with eyes;

The duck feather cape, with [a design of] young ears of maize;

The bear skin cape;

The blue knotted [cape], bordered with eyes;

The cape with a sun [design], bordered with eyes;

The old cape with the eagle head design;[13]

The cape with the war symbol;

The cape with the basket flower design;[14]

The cape with the magnolia flower design;[15]

The cape with the colored Lord's flower design;

The cape with the dahlia design;[16]

The cape with the plumeria flower design;[17]

The cape with the poinsettia design;[18]

The white duck feather cape, diagonally divided;

The white duck feather cape, with the face of a bear;

quappachtentlaiaoalo tilmatli,

coioichcatentlaiaoalo tilmatli,

quappachtlalpilli tilmatli,

colotlaxochio tilmatli,

quapachatocaio tilmatli,

quappapaloio tilmatli,

oçelotilmatli,

quauhtetepoio tilmatli,

oçeloxicalcoliuhquj tilmatli,

ocelotilmatli,

oçeloquauhtlatlapanquj tilmatli,

quappachixcoliuhquj tilmatli,

tlallecaoazio, tilmatli,

tlamachmoiaoac tilmatli,

xomoiujtilmatli tentlapallo,

xomoiujtilmatli quappatlacio,

iztac xomoiujtilmatli tenjxio

xomoiujtilmatli elotic

cujtlaichujtilmatli,

xiuhtlalpilli tenjxio,

tonatiuhio tilmatli tenjxio,

quauhtzonteconio tilmatli mamanquj,

teuatl tlachinoltilmatli,

oacalxuchio tilmatli,

eloxuchio tilmatli,

tlapaltecuxuchio tilmatli,

acucuxuchio tilmatli,

cacaloxuchio tilmatli,

cuetlaxxuchio tilmatli,

iztac xomoiujtilmatli nacazmjnquj,

iztac xomoiujtilmatli cujtlachixio,

---

11. *Oçeloxicalcoliuhquj* (*ocelotl, xicalli, coliuhqui*—ocelot, gourd, twisted): gourd vessel with curved decoration. The nature of weaving makes it a stepped design.

12. Cf. representation in *Primeros memoriales*, Cap. IV.

In the *Real Academia de la Historia MS*, *yapalixcoliuhqui tilmatli* follows *quappachixcoliuhqui tilmatli*.

13. Cf. Sahagún, *op. cit.*, I, p. 161 (*quauhtzontli*).

14. Pannier flower design, in Eduard Seler: *Collected Works* (J. Eric S. Thompson and Francis B. Thompson, eds.; Cambridge, Mass.: Carnegie Institution of Washington, 1939), Vol. II, Part 3, p. 95 (*Anthurium* sp.?). Emily Walcott Emmart, in *The Badianus Manuscript* (*Codex Barberini, Latin 241*) (Baltimore: The Johns Hopkins Press, 1940), p. 234, calling it a basket flower, says it is a species of *xanthosoma*. Francisco de Santamaría, in *Diccionario general de americanismos* (Méjico: Editorial Pedro Robredo, 1942), II, p. 102, identifies the *huacalsóchil* (*-súchil*) as *Phyllodendron affine*, Hemsl.

15. Seler, *op. cit.*, p. 96 (*Magnolia* sp.?). Emmart, *op. cit.*, p. 275, mentions another *eloxochitl* belonging to the *Compositae*.

Yolloxochiotilmatli, here listed in the *Real Academia de la Historia MS*, is omitted in the *Florentine Codex*.

16. In Francisco Hernández: *Historia de las plantas de Nueva España* (México: Imprenta Universitaria, 1942), I, p. 24, this is *Dahlia coccinea* Cav.; in Seler, *loc. cit.*, *D. variabilis*; in Emmart, *op. cit.*, p. 305, *Dahlia* sp.

17. In Hernández, *op. cit.*, III, p. 806, *Plumeria acutifolia* Poir; in Seler, *loc. cit.*, *P. rubra*; in Emmart, *op. cit.*, p. 308, *P. rubra* L. Santamaría, *op. cit.*, I, p. 251, identifies the *cacalosúchil* as *P. rubra* L., *P. bicolor* R. & P., and *P. acutifolia* Poir. Cecile Hulse Matschat, in *Mexican Plants for American Gardens* (Boston and New York: Houghton Mifflin Company, 1935), pp. 23, 177, has *P. acuminata*, and refers to it as "frangipani" and "temple flower."

18. In Hernández, *op. cit.*, III, p. 958, *Euphorbia (Poinsettia) pulcherrima* Willd; in Seler, *loc. cit.*, *Poinsettia pulcherrima*.

The cape of colored feathers, with embroidery;

The cape with the face of a bear;

The cape with the tips of eagle wings;

The cape with a border of popcorn flowers;

The cape with the ivy design;[19]

The bed covering cape;

The mattress;[20]

The large cape used to keep oneself dry;

The breech clout with the ivy design embroidered at the ends;[21]

The breech clout with the market place design;

The breech clout with the eagle's leg design;

The breech clout with the turquoise mosaic mirror design;

The breech clout with the butterfly design at the ends;[21]

The breech clout striped in many colors;

The breech clout made of twenty pieces,[22] with the wind jewel design at the ends;[21]

The tawny colored breech clout with embroidered ends;

The carmine-colored breech clout with the ocelot head;

The ocelot breech clout with a step design;

The coyote fur [breech clout] with the eagle head;[23]

The breech clout with feathered discs at the ends;

The breech clout with radiating embroidery at the ends.

tlapaliujtilmatli tlamachio,

cujtlachixio tilmatli,

quauhaaujtzoio tilmatli,

tenjzqujxuchio tilmatli,

quaxoxotilmatli,

vevej tilmatli pepechtli,

quachpepechtli,

vevej tilmatli neoatzalonj,

quaxoxoacatlamachio maxtlatl,

tianqujzio maxtlatl,

quauhtetepoio maxtlatl,

xiuhtezcaio maxtlatl,

acapapaloio maxtlatl,

centzonmaxtlatl tlatlatlapalpoalli,

cempoalçotl acahecacozcaio,

quappachmaxtlatl acan tlamachio,

nochpalmaxtlatl, ocelotzontecoio

oceloxicalcoliuhquj maxtlatl,

quauhtzontecoio,

acaiujtemalacaio maxtlatl,

acatlamachmoiaoac maxtlatl.

---

19. Sahagún, *op. cit.*, III, p. 257.

20. *Vevej tilmatli pepechtli; quachpepechtli:* cf. Alonso de Molina: *Vocabulario de la lengua mexicana* (Julio Platzmann, ed.; Leipzig: B. G Teubner, 1880), Spanish-Nahuatl section—*alhombra, colchon.*

21. Seler, *op. cit.*, p. 97, reads *yaca-* for *aca-.*

22. Cf. Spanish text, fol. 16*v.*

23. The *Florentine Codex* omits *coyoichcamaxtlatl* before *quauhtzontecoio,* found in the *Real Academia de la Historia MS.*

Ninth Chapter, in which is told that with which the rulers were arrayed when they danced.

The [head] band with [two] quetzal feather[1] tassels set off with gold, with which they bound their hair;

A quetzal feather crest device set off with gold, which he bore upon his back;

A finely wrought headdress of red spoonbill[2] feathers, with flaring quetzal feathers, and with it a drum [covered] with gold—a device which he bore upon his back as he danced;

A golden arm band;[3]

Golden ear plugs, which he inserted [in the lobes of his ears];

A wrist band of cured leather, on which was a large, round, green stone or a fine turquoise which he placed on his wrist; [it was] treated with Peru balsam, so that it gleamed;

A green stone lip plug set in gold;

A long, white labret of clear crystal, shot through with blue cotinga[4] feathers, in a gold setting, which he inserted in his [lower] lip;

A long, yellow labret of amber in a gold setting;

A long, curved, green stone labret, fitted at the base in a gold setting;

A gold lip pendant;

A gold lip pendant in the form of a pelican;[5]

A gold lip pendant in the form of an eagle;[6]

A gold lip pendant in the form of a fire serpent;

A gold lip pendant in the form of a boating pole;

A disc-shaped lip plug of fine turquoise in a gold setting;[7]

A curved, green stone lip plug in a gold setting;

A green stone lip plug in the form of an eagle, fitted at the base in a gold setting;

Injc chicunauj capitulo vncan moteneoa injn nechichioaia in tlatoque in jcoac maceoaia.

Quetzallalpilonj, coztic teocujtlaio injc qujlpiaia, intzon

quetzalpatzactli, coztic teocujtlaio in qujmama

tlauhquetzoltzontlj tlaçotlanquj, quetzalli icuecuetlacacaio, iujcal ueuetl coztic teocujtlaio, in tlaujztli in qujmama mjtotia

teucujtlamatemecatl, coztic
teocujtlanacochtli coztic in caquja

matzopetztli in cuetlaxtli, vej chalchiujtl ololiuhquj, anoço vej teuxiujtl ipan ca in jmaquechtlan qujtlalia ujtziloxitica injc tlachiuhtli injc tlapetzolli

chalchiuhtentetl coztic teucujtlatica callo,
iztac teçacatl, xiuhtototica tlamjntli, iztac teujlotl in jntenco caquja, coztic teucujtlatl in jcallo.

Coztic teçacatl, in apoçonalli teucujtlatica tlacallotilli,
chalchiuhteçacanecujlli, coztic teucujtlatl ic tlatzincallotilli,
teucujtlatempilolli coztic
atototempilolli coztic teucujtlatl,
quauhtempilolli coztic teucujtlatl,
xiuhcoatempilolli coztic teucujtlatl,
aujctempilolli coztic teucujtlatl,
temalacatentetl teuxiujtl coztic teucujtlatl icallo,

chalchiuhtencololli, coztic teucujtlatl icallo,
chalchiuhquauhtentetl, coztic teucujtlatl itzincallo,

---

1. Clark, *op. cit.,* II, p. 112, identifies *quetzaltototl* as *Pharomachrus mocinno mocinno.*
2. *Platalea ajaja* L. (Seler, *op. cit.,* p. 124).
3. One such is described more fully in Anderson and Dibble, *op. cit.,* II, p. 67.
4. Clark, *op. cit.,* p. 134, identifies blue cotinga as *Cotinga amabilis.*
5. Cf. Seler, *op. cit.,* p. 102.
6. *Quauhtentetl: quauh* could mean warrior; elsewhere we always give preference to the meaning *eagle.*
7. After this phrase, the *Real Academia de la Historia MS* has *chalchiuhtemalacatentetl coztic teucuitlatl ycallo*—a large, circular lip plug of green stone in a gold setting.

A lip pendant of gold, in the form of a broad-leafed water plant;

A crescent-shaped lip pendant of gold;

A green stone nose rod;

A fine turquoise nose rod;

A necklace of round, green stones, joined and strung together;

A necklace of radiating golden pendants with a thin, green stone [disc] set in their midst;[8]

A finely wrought feather arm band with various [other] costly feathers and with gold;

A golden band for the calf of the leg;

A quetzal feather banner held in the hand;

A quetzal bird as headdress;

Quetzal feather horns;

A quetzal feather fan [set] with gold;

A turquoise [mosaic] wrist band with a conical extension;

A necklace of gold [beads] and small sea shells;

A necklace of gold [beads] and snail shells;

Flowers and tobacco, [which were] exclusively the ruler's; a mirror in which the ruler looked at himself when he adorned himself. All these were the charge of the artisans[9] when the ruler danced.

Sandals of ocelot skin; cured leather sandals with embroidery—embroidered sandals.

[There were] two-toned drums and supports for two-toned drums, ground drums, golden gourd rattles,[10] and golden bells;

Singers, a dancer, a player of two-toned drums and one of ground drums, a drum beater, a singer who intoned the chant.

[There were] chests for the devices, in which were kept all which have been described: a large basket-case in which were kept the green stone lip plugs, the gold ear plugs, the golden necklaces, the wigs, the masks, the golden reed serpent.

There were flowering trees, which were to be seen in the palace courtyard; for it was the ruler who was to dance.

[There were] a basket for the mirror, a basket for the comb; and a rubber hammer with which the two-toned drum was sounded.

apatlactempilolli, coztic teucujtlatl,

metztempilolli coztic teucujtlatl,
chalchiuhiacamjtl,
teuxiuhiacamjtl,
chalchiuhcozcatl ololiuhquj, tlacenqujxtilli, tlaçe-cotl,
coztic teucujtlachaiaoac cozcatl, chalchiuhtlacana-oalli iitic manj,
quetzalmachoncotl tlaçotlanquj nepapan tlaçoiuj-tica, ioan coztic teucujtlaio,
coztic teucujtlacotzeoatl,
quetzalmacpanjtl,
quetzaltotoicpacxuchitl,
quetzalquaquaujtl,
quetzalecaceoaztli coztic teucujtlaio
xiuhmacopilli,

coztic teucujtlachipulcozcatl,
teucujtlacoztic acuechcozcatl,
xuchitl, ietl, ineiscaujl tlatoanj, tezcatl injc motta tlatoanj, injc muchichioa amanteca impial, in isqujch imaçeoaia tlatoanj,

oçeloeoacactli, cuetlaxcactli tlamachio, tlamachcac-tli,
teponaztli, teponaztzatzaztli, veuetl aiacachtli coz-tic teucujtlatl, tetzilacatl coztic teucujtlatl,

cujcanjme, mjtotianj, teponaçoanj, ueuetzonanj, tlatzotzonquj, cujcaitoanj,

tlaujzpetlacalli, in vncan mopiaia, in ixqujch omjto. Veuej toptanatli, in vncan mopia, in chal-chiuhtentetl, in teucujtlanacochtli, in teucujtlacoz-catl, tzoncalli, xaiacatl, teucujtlaacaçoatl coztic teu-cujtlatl,

xuchiquaujtl momanaia, in tecpan itoalco, inezca catca: ca maçeoaz in tlatoanj,

tezcatanatli, tziquaoaztanatli, olmaitl injc motzo-tzona teponaztli.

8. Cf. Seler, *Gesammelte Abhandlungen*, II, p. 542; also corresponding Spanish text.
9. Cf. Sahagún, *op. cit.*, II, pp. 389ff, on etymology of *amanteca*.
10. Corresponding Spanish text: *"vnas sonajas de oro."*

Tenth Chapter, in which is told how the rulers took their pleasure.

When the ruler went forth, in his hand rested his reed stalk which he went moving in rhythm with his words. His chamberlains and his elders went before him; on both sides, on either hand, they proceeded as they went clearing the way for him. None might cross in front of him; none might come forth before him; none might look up at him; none might come face to face with him.

He sang; songs were learned; chants were intoned. They told him proverbs and pleasantries to pass the time.

They played ball. There were his ball-catchers and his ball-players. They wagered [in this game] all [manner of] costly goods—gold, golden necklaces, green stone, fine turquoise, slaves,[1] precious capes, valuable breech clouts, cultivated fields, houses, leather leg bands, gold bracelets, arm bands of quetzal feathers, duck feather capes, bales of cacao— [these] were wagered there in the game called *tlachtli.*

On the two sides, on either hand, it was limited by walls, very well made, in that the walls and floor were smoothed. And there, in the very center of the ball court, was a line, drawn upon the ground. And on the walls were two stone, ball court rings. He who played caused [the ball] to enter there; he caused it to go in. Then he won all the costly goods, and he won everything from all who watched there in the ball court. His equipment was the rubber ball, the leather gloves, girdles, and leather hip guards.

Patolli was played with large beans—four large beans with holes bored into the surfaces. The game was won when from their hands they scattered the four beans on a mat painted in widely spaced black [lines], with which the *patolli* mat was designed. There went to be added the counters—twelve [of them], six the property of each, the counters of each of the contenders. He who won in playing *patolli,*

Injc matlactli capitulo, ipan mjtoa injc meellel-qujxtiaia tlatoque.

In jcoac qujça tlatoanj, imac onotiuh, iacapitzac, injc mapilotiuh, injc matlatotiuh qujiacana in jtechiuhcaoan, in jtaoan, necoc vmac in mantiuj, in qujtlapeujlitiuj: aiac vel qujiacaujltequj, aiac uel ixpan qujça, aiac vel acopa qujtta, aiac uel qujxnepanoa,

cujca, mocujcamachtia, cujcaeheooa, qujtlatlaquechilia, qujçaçanjlhuja,

vllama, vncatca imolpixcaoa, ioan inmolancaoan, qujtlanjtoa in jxqujch tlaçotli in teucujtlatl, in teocujtlacozcatl, in chalchiujtl, in teuxiujtl, in tlaçotli, in tlaçotilmatli, in tlaçomaxtlatl, in mjlli, in callj, cotzehoatl, teucujtlamatemecatl, quetzalmachoncotl, xomoiujtilmatli, cacaoapetlatl in vncan netlanjoa, itoca tlachtli:

necocampa imac tlatepantectli, cenca tlaiecchiuhtli injc xipetztic in tlachmatl, ioan in tlalmantli: auh in vncan vel inepantla tlachtli, onoca tlecotl tlaxotlalli in tlalli, auh in jtech tlachmatl, vntetl tlachtemalacatl manca, in aqujn ollamanj vncan tlacalaquja, vncan qujcalaquja olli: njman ic qujtlanj in jxqujch tlaçotli tlatqujtl, auh muchintin qujntlanj, in jxqujchtin tetlatlattaque, in vncan tlachco: itlaujcallo in olli, maieoatl, nelpilonj, queçeoatl.

Patoa ica aiecotli, vevej etl nauhtetl in tlaixcoionjlli injc motlanj immatica in qujchaiaoa in nauhtetl etl, qujcujloa ce petlatl, tliltica, papatlactic in tlilli, injc mjcujloa patolpetlatl, in vncan mopouhtiuh tlapoaltetl matlactetl omome chichiquacentetl imaxca intlapoalteuh icecemme in jxnamjquj in motlanj in patoa, qujtlanjlia in ixqujch tlaçotli, coztic teucujtlacozcatl, chalchiujtl, teuxiujtl, matzopetztli ipan ca chalchiujtl

---

1. *Tlaçotli:* the corresponding Spanish has slaves (*tlacotli*). See also below, description of *patolli.*

won[2] all the costly goods: golden necklaces, green stone, fine turquoise, bracelets on which were round, green stones or fine turquoise, quetzal feathers, slaves, houses, fields, precious capes, mats, large capes, green stone lip plugs, golden ear plugs, duck feather capes. And he who played *patolli,* who cast the beans, if then he made one [of them] stand, if the bean stood up there on its thicker end, it was taken as a great omen; it was regarded as a great marvel. Then he won all the costly goods. [The other] lost even though he had not yet attained the specified number of throws. Thus were all agreed; thus all came to the end [of the game].

They shot with bow and arrow—with a bow, with a shaft, with bird arrows, with darts. With this belonged a bracelet on which were large, round, green stones or fine turquoises. The ruler placed it about his wrist.

They used a blowgun. They shot pellets with the blowgun.[3] With it belonged a pellet bag [where clay pellets were stored and a tubular copper hook] to remove the pellets. They shot small birds with it. They hunted with a bird net; with it they captured various birds.

Flower gardens were laid out; flower beds were laid out. They put in them all the various flowers.

There were their jesters who provided them solace and gave them pleasure. And [there were those] who rolled a log with their feet thus bringing pleasure in many ways. Their deeds were laughable and marvelous; for with the soles of his feet one man [lying] below this did—he made a thick, round log dance with the soles of his feet [while] he lay upon his back and cast the log upward. With only the soles of his feet he did this.

Many things they did to bring men pleasure. There were their servants, their pages who attended them and gave them solace; dwarfs, cripples, hunchbacks, servants. They kept eagles, ocelots, bears, mountain cats, and various birds.

ololiuhquj anoço teuxiujtl, quetzalli, tlacotli, calli, mjlli, tlaçotilmatli, pepechtli, veuej tilmatli: chalchiuhtentetl, teucujtlanacochtli, xomoiujtilmatli. Auh in aqujn patoanj, in qujchaiaoa in etl, intla centetl etl ic teequechili, in moquetzticaz etl, in vmpa ic tzinmjjltic: cenca tetzammachoia, cenca tlamaujçolli ipan mottaia: njman muchi qujtlanj, in jxqujch tlaçotli, in motlanjtoa in macanel aiamo açi in quezqujtetl aqujlli, injc netennonotzalo, injc netzopalo.

Tlatlamjna tlaujtoltica, tipontica, totomjtica, tlacochtica: itlaujcallo, matzopetztli ipan ca, uej chalchiujtl, ololiuhquj, anoço teuxiujtl in jmaquechtlan qujtlalia tlatoanj.

Tlatlacaloazuja, tlatlamotla ican tlacalhoaztli, iujcallo telolmatlatl [yn oncã mopia çoquitelolotli, yoan tepozcocotli] mjmjltic injc mopetlaoa telolotli, ic qujmotla tepitoton totome, tlatlapechmatlauja in jca totomatlatl: injc qujmaçi nepapan totome,

moxochimjltia, moxochitepantia, caquja, in jxqujch nepapan xochitl,

vncatca intetlaveuetzqujticahoan in qujmellelqujxtiaia, in qujcecemeltia: ioan quaujlacatzoque in qujpaqujltia mjiec tlamantli in jntlachioal teuetzqujti, ioan maujztic, in jca ixocpal tlanjpa injc tlâmati çe tlacatl, tomaoac in quanmjmjlli in qujtotia ica ixocpal aqueztoc acopa in conmaiauj quammjmjlli ça iehoatl in jxocpal ic tlamati,

mjiec tlamãtli, in tececemelti in qujchioa, vncatca imaachoan, ixoloan in qujnujcatinenca in qujmehellelqujxtiaia, tzapame, villame, tepotzome, teachme, qujnpiaia quaquauhti, oçelome, cujcujtlachtin, ocotochtin, nepapan tototl.

2. The *Real Academia de la Historia MS* reads *quitlanitoa* (he wagered) instead of *qujtlanjlia.*

3. In the *Real Academia de la Historia MS* a passage appears which is not in the *Florentine Codex.* Because it changes the sense to a degree, it is here inserted in brackets.

Eleventh Chapter. Here it is told what the rulers rested upon.

The ocelot skin seat with a back rest; the mountain lion skin seat with a back rest; the bear skin seat with a back rest; the mountain cat skin seat with a back rest; the cured leather seat with a back rest; the ocelot skin seat, the mountain lion skin seat, the bear skin seat, the cured leather seat, the mountain cat[1] skin seat, the coyote skin seat.

The ocelot skin mat,[2] the mountain lion skin mat, the mountain cat skin mat, the coyote skin mat, the hammock, smooth reed mats[3] elaborately painted with designs; seats with backs, painted with designs; low seats painted with designs.

Injc matlactli oçe capitulo: vncan mjtoa, in jpan motlaliaia tlatoque.

Oçeloeoatepotzoicpalli, mjçeoatepotzoicpalli, cujtlacheoatepotzoicpalli, ocotocheoatepotzoicpalli, cuetlaxtepotzoicpalli, oçeloeoaicpalli, mjçeoaicpalli, cujtlacheoaicpalli, cuetlaxicpalli, ocotocheoaicpalli, coioeoaicpalli,

oçeloeoapepechtli, mjçeoapepechtli, ocotocheoapepechtli, coioeoapepechtli, cochizmatlatl alaoacapetlatl, tlatlacujlolli, tepotzoicpalli tlacujlolli, tzinjcpalli tlacujlolli.

---

1. Cf. Sahagún, *op. cit.*, III, p. 153.
2. *Pepechtli:* cf. corresponding Spanish text.
3. *Alauacapetlatl:* corresponding Spanish text—*"vnos petates muy pintados y muy curiosos."*

Twelfth Chapter, in which it is told how the rulers were arrayed whom they sent to the wars.

The costly red spoonbill headdress set off with gold, having very many quetzal feathers flaring [from it], and with it, borne upon his back, the skin drum upon a carrying frame, and decorated with gold.

And they dressed him in a red shirt, made of red spoonbill feathers [decorated with] flint knives[1] [fashioned of] gold; and his *sapote* leaf skirt was made all of quetzal feathers.

The shield was ringed with thin gold, and its pendants were made of precious feathers.[2]

[He had] a green stone necklace of round, large, green stone and fine turquoise combined.

The ruler placed upon his head a blue cotinga feather headdress which was set off with gold, and had quetzal feathers flaring [from it]. Over the upper part of his body he put a shirt of blue cotinga feathers.

And as a burden for his back [he had] a blue skin drum fashioned on a frame, and [ornamented] with gold.[3]

All quetzal feathers was its *sapote* skirt; and its pendants were all costly feathers. And the [ornaments of] flint knives, for its covering of blue cotinga feathers, were of thin gold [plate].

The ocelot Xipe was made of ocelot skin; its flint knife [decoration] was made of gold.

Its *sapote* leaf skirt was all of quetzal feathers.

The ocelot drum, the burden on his back, was of gold [decorated] with [wavy lines called] hawk scratches.

The shield was covered with blue cotinga feathers and had a disc of gold in the center.

Injc matlactlomome capitulo, vncan mjtoa: injc muchichioaia in tlatoque, in qujtitlanja iaupan.

Tlauhquecholtzontli tlaçotlanquj coztic teucujtlaio: cenca mjiec in quetzalli icuecuetlacacaio: iujcal in tlamamalli, veuetl in colotli tlachiuhtli, coztic teucujtlaio:

auh in iehoatl commaquja tlatlauhquj, tlauhquecholiujtl injc tlachiuhtli: coztic teucujtlatl in jtetecpaio, auh in jtzapocue mochiuhtoc çan moch quetzalli.

Chimalli, coztic teucujtlatl, in tlatzotzontli imanaoaio, tlaçoiujtl in jtentlapilollo muchiuhtoc,

chalchiuhcozcatl, tlacenqujxtilli in ololiuhquj, in veuej, chalchiujtl, ioan teuxiujtl

xiuhtototzontli, coztic teucujtlaio, quetzalli in jcuecuetlacacaio, in jtzontecon conmaquja tlatoanj: auh in jtlac conaquja xiuhtotoeoatl,

auh in tlamamalli xoxouhquj veuetl in colotli tlachiuhtli coztic teucujtlaio

çan much quetzalli in jtzapocue, mochi tlaçoiujtl in jtlapilollo, coztic teucujtlatl in tlacanaoalli in jtetecpaio, in xiuhtotoeoatl,

ocelototec, oçeloeoatl injc tlachiuhtli, coztic teucujtlatl injc tlachiuhtli in jtetecpaio,

ça much quetzalli in jtzapocue,

oçeloueuetl in tlamamalli coztic teucujtlatl injc tlotloujtequj.

Chimalli xiuhtototica tzacquj, coztic teucujtlatl ic itixapo,

---

1. *Tetecpaio*: the corresponding Spanish text refers to *rayos de oro* where our translation uses "flint knives." The shape of the *rayo* is similar to that of a knife. Cf. also Siméon, *op. cit.*, and Seler, *op. cit.*, II, p. 594, where *Steinmesser* is used consistently.

2. The *Real Academia de la Historia MS* follows *muchiuhtoc* with *ça muchi quetzalli yn iacachapollo mochiuhtoc*—pure quetzal feathers, to which small grasshoppers [of gold] are added at the points.

3. The corresponding Spanish text reads: *"Y colgaua deste plumaje, hazia las espaldas, vn atambor pequeñuelo, puesto en vna escaleruela, como para lleuar carga."* This passage Seler (*op. cit.*, II, p. 594) translates as *"Dazu wird auf den Rücken eine Trommel getragen, aus einem Gestell bestehend, das mit Gold überzogen ist."*

The quetzal feather butterfly was the burden for the back; with it belonged the yellow parrot feather shirt, [decorated] with hawk scratches in gold.

The shield with a golden disc had a golden butterfly in the middle. [There was] a quetzal feather claw,[4] with gold. The shirt [which belonged to this] was of yellow parrot feathers.

The golden hood had horns of quetzal feathers; its shirt was of yellow parrot feathers.

The silver hood had quetzal feather tufts held in cups. With it belonged a shirt of yellow parrot feathers with hawk scratch [decorations] in gold.

[There were] the quetzal feather banner of the spear house; the silver banner with a spray of quetzal feathers held in a cup at the top; and the golden banner with a spray of quetzal feathers held in a cup at the top.

The finely wrought obsidian butterfly was of quetzal feathers and gold; its teeth and claws were all of precious feathers; and it had quetzal feather horns.

The finely wrought butterfly of [the goddess] Xochiquetzal [was made of] precious feathers; and its horns were of gold and quetzal feathers.

[There was] a quetzal feather crest-like device. With it belonged a blue cotinga-feather shirt; the shield was covered with blue cotinga feathers and had a disc of gold in the center.

The Xolotl head of yellow parrot feathers, with balls of quetzal feathers, was ornamented with gold. With it belonged a shirt of yellow parrot feathers with hawk scratch decorations in gold.

The blue Xolotl head was ornamented with quetzal feathers and gold. With it belonged a blue shirt.

The white Xolotl head was ornamented with quetzal feathers and gold. With it belonged a white shirt.

The bright red Xolotl head was ornamented with quetzal feathers and gold; its shirt was likewise bright red.

The headdress of trupial feathers was ornamented with quetzal feathers and gold. With it belonged a shirt of yellow parrot feathers.

The yellow demon of the air was made all of gold, and had quetzal feathers and balls of quetzal feathers.

The blue demon of the air had quetzal feathers, was made all of gold, and had balls of quetzal feathers.

quetzalpapalotl in tlamamalli, inamjc toçeoatl, coztic teucujtlatl injc tlotloujtecquj.

Chimalli teocujtlatica itixapo, teucujtlapapalotl ijtic manj quetzalxopilli, coztic teucujtlaio, toçeoatl in jeoaio.

Coztic teucujtlaquacalalatli, iquetzalquaquauh, ieoaio coztic toçeoatl.

Iztac teucujtlaquacalalatli, quetzaltecomaio: inamjc toçeoatl coztic teucujtlatl ic tlotloujtecquj

quetzalpanjtl tlacochcalcaiotl. Iztac teucujtlapanjtl, quetzaltzontecomaio. Coztic teucujtlapanjtl, quetzaltzontecomaio.

Itzpapalotl tlaçotlanquj quetzallo, coztic teucujtlaio, in jtlan, in jizti muchi tlaçoiujtl: iquetzalquaquauh.

Xochiquetzalpapalotl, tlaçotlanquj in tlaçoiujtica: ioan coztic teucujtlaio, iquetzalquaquauh

quetzalpatzactli, xiuhtotoeoatl iujcallo in chimalli xiuhtototica tzacquj, coztic teucujtlatl ic itixapo,

tozquaxolotl iquetzaltemal, coztic teucujtlaio, toçehoatl inamjc, coztic teucujtlatl injc motlotloujtec,

xoxouhquj quaxolotl, quetzallo coztic teucujtlaio in jnamjc xoxouhquj eoatl.

Iztac quaxolotl, quetzallo, coztic teucujtlaio in jnamjc iztac eoatl.

Chichiltic quaxolotl, quetzallo, coztic teucujtlaio, in jeoaio, çan no chichiltic.

Çaquantzontli, quetzallo, coztic teucujtlaio toçeoatl inamjc,

toztzitzimjtl: muchi coztic teucujtlatl injc tlachiuhtli, quetzallo, iquetzaltemal.

Xoxouhquj tzitzimjtl, quetzallo, muchi coztic teucujtlatl injc tlachiuhtli, iquetzaltemal.

---

4. Cf. discussion in Seler, *op. cit.*, II, pp. 598ff., as well as corresponding Spanish text—"*a manera de choça, y en toda la orilla tenja vnas flocaduras, de pluma rica, y con oro.*"

The white demon of the air was of gold, and had quetzal feather balls.

The yellow, Huaxtec, pointed, conical cap had a golden [disc] in front and was girt with quetzal feathers. And the shirt was of yellow parrot feathers [decorated with] hawk scratches. Gold was his crescent-shaped nose plate; gold were his ear pendants, with quetzal feather spindles.

The white, Huaxtec, pointed, conical, paper cap had quetzal feathers bound at the base and a [disc] of gold at the front; its spindles were of quetzal feathers and gold. Gold was his crescent-shaped nose plate, and gold were his ear pendants.

[For] the bi-colored Huaxtec, the shirt was half blue and half yellow. His conical, pointed cap was also bi-colored—half blue and half yellow, and it had quetzal feathers girt at the base and a golden [disc] at the front. Gold was his crescent-shaped nose plate; his ear pendants were gold; and his spindles were of quetzal feathers.

The golden conical cap had quetzal feather tufts held in cups. The silver conical cap had quetzal feather tufts held in cups.

[There were] shell trumpets and clay pipes which were blown in battle so that the warriors might set forth together to fight. The standard, [which was] of gold, and the quetzal feather banner dispatched the men to battle. When it was seen that already all the standards were raised, then the warriors set forth together to do battle.

The quetzal feather sun [consisted of] a golden sun, and in the middle of it was a circle of quetzal feathers. The young maize flower crest had, as its leaves, quetzal feathers, and [was ornamented] with flint knives [fashioned of] gold. On his temples went plate-like pieces of gold. The wooden sword [was provided] with obsidian blades [set in] a groove at its edge. The headdress of quetzal and heron feathers [ornamented] with gold, [had] single quetzal feathers, and many quetzal feathers rustled [from it. There was] the ocelot wine jar, whose foam had single quetzal feathers [set in it], and many quetzal feathers rustled [from it].

Iztac tzitzimjtl, coztic teucujtlaio, iquetzaltemal.

Coztic cuextecatl icopil ujtzauhquj, ixquateucujtlaio, quetzaltica cujtlalpic: auh in eoatl, toçeoatl motlotloujtec, coztic teucujtlatl in jiacametz, ipipilol, coztic teucujtlatl, imamalacaquetzal.

Iztac cuextecatl iamacal ujtzauhquj, quetzaltica cujtlalpic, ixquateucujtlaio, imamalacaquetzal teucujtlaio: coztic teucujtlatl in jiacametz, ipipilol coztic teucujtlatl.

Chictlapanquj cuextecatl, çectlapal xoxouhquj, cectlapal coztic in eoatl, icopil ujtzauhquj, no chictlapanquj, cectlapal xoxouhquj, cectlapal coztic quetzaltica cujtlalpic, ixquateucujtlaio, coztic teucujtlatl in jiacametz, ipipilol coztic teucujtlatl, imamalacaquetzal.

Coztic teucujtlacopilli quetzaltecomaio. Iztac teucujtlacopilli, quetzaltecomaio,

tlapitzalli tecuçiztli, ioan qujqujztli in mopitza iauc injc çemeoa iauqujzque, injc mjcali: in quachpanjtl, coztic teucujtlapanjtl: ioan quetzalpanjtl in teeujtia in iauc, in omottac ie meoatiquetza in jzquj quachpanjtl. Niman çemeoa in iauqujzque, injc mjcali,

quetzaltonatiuh, coztic teucujtlatl in tonatiuh ijtic mantiuh in quetzalli iaoaltic. Xiloxochipatzactli, quetzalli in jizoaio, coztic teucujtlatl in jtecpaio, in jcanaoacãn mamantiuh: coztic teucujtlatl in tlacomaltectli. Maquaujtl itztzo in jtenco tlatectli, quetzalaztatzontli, teucujtlaio, quetzalxixilquj: auh in jcuecuetlacacaio mjiec quetzalli, oçelotlachicomjtl, in jpoçonca quetzalxixilquj: auh in jcuecuetlacacaio mjiec in quetzalli.

ILLUSTRATIONS

vn pcco, despues de la media noche
y llegaua hasta la mañana la luz
del sol la encubria. De manera
que saliendo el sol, no parecia mas
segun algunos, viose vn año ente-
ro, y segun otros, quatro años arreo.
Quando aparecia de noche esta
cometa, todos los yndios, dauan
grandissimos alaridos, y se espan-
tauan esperando, que algun
gran mal auia de venir.

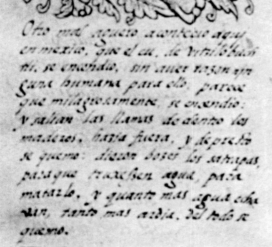

Otro mal aguero acontecio aqui
en mexico, que el cu, de vitzilobuchtli, se encendio, sin auer razon nin-
guna humana para ello, parece
que milagrosamente, se encendio:
y saltan las llamas de dentro los
maderos, hazia fuera, y de presto
se quemo: dieron bozes los satrapas
para que traxessen agua, para
matarlo, y quanto mas agua echa-
uan, tanto mas ardia, del todo se
quemo.

hitic illaquitl, vel illhuipa tollontocac
achitic inuic ittoia: vmpa ilap-
copa moaltzoquetzaia, ciuh onqui-
iolitzepontia, invecua tlathuilia
ia, ipan tlathuja. Quinichoatl
quioalpoloaia, motonaliuh, injoac
oalquiçaia: uel cexiuitl moatmo
quetzaia (ipan moatectlonome-
cahi inpeuh) auh injcoacnecui
tlacoaiaia, netenuitecoia, net101
uitoia, tlatemmachoia.

Injc vntetl tetzauitl mochiuh,
injan mexico, çanmonomatqui n
tlatlac tacatl(on, ciacma quipeua
cuj çanmonoma tlecuiç, injatl diablo vitzilobuchtli mitoaia
itocaiocan Tlacateca inneztetlaia
motlaquechalli itlic oalquiça intle
myiaoatl, intlenenepilli, intlecue-
çalluitl, cenca çan iuicha ompalo
mixquich oalquauitl. Niman icic
tlatoaca quitoa, Mexicae, ma
oallatotoca, tlaceuiloz, amapilol;
auh injcoac oatequiaia, injçij
ceuiznequia, çanic ilhuice mopitz
aocmouel ceuh uellatlac.

Page from *Florentine Codex* (Chapter 6).

Rulers of Tenochtitlan. 1. Acamapichtli. 2. Uitziliuitl. 3. Chimalpopoca. 4. Itzcoatl. 5. Moctezuma the Elder. 6. Axayacatl. 7. Tiçoc. 8. Auitzotl. 9. Moctezuma the Younger. 12. Quauhtemoc. 13. Don Andrés Motelchiuh. 14. Don Pablo Xochiquen. 15. Don Diego Uanitl. 16. Don Diego Teuetzquiti. 17. Don Cristóbal Cecepatic. (Chapter 1.)

10, 11. Omens observed in Tenochtitlan (Chapter 1).

Rulers of Tlatilulco. 18. Quaquapitzauac. 19. Tlacateotl. 20. Quauhtlatoa. 21. Moquiuixtli. 22. Don Pablo Temilo. 23. Don Martín Ecatl. 24. Don Juan Auelittoc. 25. Don Martín Tlacatecatl. 26. Don Diego Uitznauatlailotlac. 27. Don Alonso Quauhnochtli. (Chapter 2.)

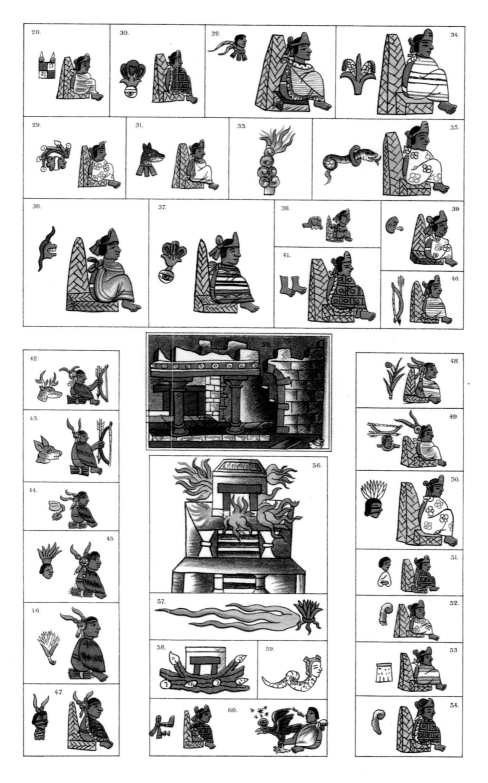

Rulers of Texcoco. 28. Tlaltecatzin. 29. Techotlalatzin. 30. Ixtlilxochitl. 31. Neçaualcoyotzin. 32. Neçaual-pilli. 34. Cacamatzin. 35. Coanacochtzin. 36. Tecocoltzin. 37. Ixtlilxochitl. 38. Yoyontzin. 39. Tetlaueuetz-quiti. 40. Don Antonio Tlauitoltzin. 41. Don Hernando Pimentel. (Chapter 3.)

33. Omens observed in Texcoco (Chapter 3).

Rulers of Uexotla. 42. Maçatzin tecutli. 43. Tochin tecutli. 44. Ayotzin tecutli. 45. Quatlauice tecutli. 46. Totomochtzin. 47. Yaotzin tecutli. 48. Xilotzin tecutli. 49. Itlacauhtzin. 50. Tlaçolyaotzin. 51. Tzonte-moctzin. 52. Cuitlauatzin. 53. Tzapocuetzin. 54. Cuitlauatzin. (Chapter 4.)

55. Tollan (Chapter 5).

Omens observed in Tenochtitlan. 56. Burning temple. 57. Comet. 58. Inundation. 59. Ciuacoatl weeping. 60. Bird with mirror on its head. (Chapter 6.)

—After Paso y Troncoso

Omens (concluded). 61. Two-headed men (Chapter 6).
62. Spaniards landing on the coast (Chapter 7). 63. Game of *patolli* (Chapter 10). 64. Rolling a log on the soles of one's feet (Chapter 10). 65. Animals kept by the ruler (Chapter 10). 66. Judgment and punishment of malefactors—Tlacxitlan (Chapter 14). 67. Same—Quauhcalco (Chapter 14). 68. Same—Tecpilcalli (Chapter 14). 69. Musicians (Chapter 14). 70. Array and equipment for the dance (Chapter 14). 71. The ruler's animals (Chapter 14).

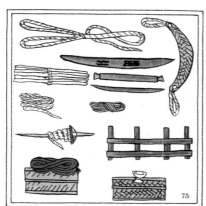

72-74. Women's array—*uipilli, cueitl* (Chapter 15). 75. Weaving and spinning equipment (Chapter 16). 76. Laying plans for war (Chapter 17). 77. The ruler's war array (Chapter 17). 78. Priests and warriors in battle array (Chapter 17).

—*After Paso y Troncoso*

79. Warriors in battle array (Chapter 17). 80. Conquest of a city (Chapter 17). 81. Sacrifice of a war captive (Chapter 17). 82-84. Judges (Chapter 17). 85. A trial (Chapter 17).

—After Paso y Troncoso

86. Punishment of an erring official (Chapter 17). 87. Punishment of a careless musician (Chapter 17). 88-90. Keeping watch in the city against enemies (Chapter 17). 91. The game *tlachtli* (Chapter 17). 92. Gifts of the ruler to the poor (Chapter 17).

—After Paso y Troncoso

93, 94. Ceremonies on election of a new ruler (Chapter 18). 95, 96. Goods displayed in the market place (Chapter 19). 97-100. Gifts of the ruler to successful warriors (Chapters 20 and 21).

Thirteenth Chapter. Here are told the foods which the lords ate.[1]

Hot, white, doubled tortillas;[2] large tortillas; large, thick, coarse tortillas; folded tortillas[2] of maize treated with lime, pleasing [to the taste]; tortillas formed in rolls; leaf-shaped tortillas;

White tamales with beans forming a sea shell on top;[3] white tamales with maize grains thrown in;[4] hard, white tamales with grains of maize thrown in; red tamales with beans forming a sea shell on top; tamales made of a dough of maize softened in lime, with beans forming a sea shell on top; tamales of maize softened in wood ashes; turkey pasty cooked in a pot, or sprinkled with seeds; tamales of meat cooked with maize and yellow chili; roast turkey hen; roast quail.

Market food: white tortillas with a flour of uncooked beans; turkey with a sauce of small chilis, tomatoes, and ground squash seeds; turkey with red chilis; turkey with yellow chilis; turkey with green chilis; venison sprinkled with seeds; hare with sauce; rabbit with sauce; meat stewed with maize, red chili, tomatoes, and ground squash seeds; venison with red chili, tomatoes, and ground squash seeds; birds with toasted maize; small birds; dried duck; duck stewed in a pot; the *atzitzicuilotl* bird stewed in a pot; roast of meat; fried meat in a sauce of red chili, tomatoes, and ground squash seeds; pottage of yellow chili; sauces of ordinary tomatoes and small tomatoes and yellow chili, or of tomatoes and green chili; diluted [sauces] with tomatoes; white fish with yellow chili; grey fish with red chili, tomatoes, and ground squash seeds; frog with green chilis; newt with yellow chili; tadpoles with small chilis; small fish with small chilis; winged ants with savory

Ic matlactli vmej capitulo: vncan mjtoa, in jntlaqual in qujquaia, in tlatoque.

Iztac totonquj tlaxcalli, tlacuelpacholli, vei tlaxcalli quauhtlaqualli, tlaxcalpacholli iztac, nexiopapaio, tlaxcalmjmjlli, tlacepoalli tlaxcalli,

quatecujcujlli tamalli, iztac tlatzincujtl, iztac tetamalli tlatzincujtl, chichiltic quatecujcujlli tamalli, nexiotamalli quatecujcujlli, tamalatl quauhnextli, totolnacaqujmjlli xocco tlapaoaxtli, anoço tlatentli, nacatlaoio tamalli chilcozio: cihoatototli tlatleoatzalli, çolin tlatleoatzalli,

tianqujztlaqualli, iztac tlaxcalli etica tlaoio, totolin patzcalmolli, chiltecpiio, totolin, chilcozio totolin, chilchoio totolin, maçanacatl tlatentli, citli molli, tochtli molli, nacatlaolli patzcallo, maçanacatl patzcallo, totoizqujtl tepitoton totome, canauhtlaoatzalli, canauhtlapaoaxtli, atzitzicujlotlapaoaxtli, nacatlacectli, tlatetzoionjlli nacamolli patzcallo, chilcoztlatonjlli, chiltecpinmolli xitomaio, chilcozmolli xitomaio, chilchomolli xitomaio, tlamamollalli xitomaio, iztac amjlotl chilcozio, tomaoac xoujli, patzcallo, cujatl chilchoio, axolotl chilcozio, atepocatl chiltecpiio, mjchpili chiltecpijo, tzicatanatli inamjc papaloqujlitl, chapolin chichiaoa, meocujli chiltecpinmollo, chacali patzcallo, topotli mjchi patzcallo, tlacamjchin patzcallo, maçaxocomolli iztac mjchio

---

1. Sahagún's Spanish sometimes varies somewhat from dictionary and other definitions of the foods named in the Aztec text. In the main, our translation favors Sahagún's; footnotes take account of the most noticeable variations.

2. *Tlacuelpacholli, tlaxcalpacholli:* hot, white tortillas, doubled, arranged in a large basket, according to the corresponding Spanish text. In Molina, *op. cit.,* the word means *"cosa doblada, o plegada."*—If the root of *-pacholli* is *pachoa,* the term could indicate that the tortillas were covered, or could refer to the way they were beaten out. See also note 3, *infra.*

3. In Sahagún, *op. cit.,* III, p. 367, Dr. Ignacio Alcocer translates *quatecuicuilli tamali patzcalmoli inamic* as *Tamales de caracol encima y mole exprimido juntos.* Álvaro Tezozomoc, in *Histoire du Mexique* (tr. Ternaux-Compans; Paris: P. Janet, 1853), I, p. 269, has this explanation: *"les mets appelés* quatequicuil-tamalli, hurey-tlacalli [hueuey tlaxcalli?], tlaxcatl-pacholli, *grands gâteaux de farine de fève et de farine de maïs qui ont deux palmes d'épaisseur, ainsi que tout espèce d'oiseaux et de gibier."*

4. Cf. Molina, *op. cit.*

herbs;[5] locusts with chía; maguey grubs with a sauce of small chilis; lobster with red chili, tomatoes, and ground squash seeds; sardines[6] with red chili, tomatoes, and ground squash seeds; large fish with the same; a sauce of unripened plums with white fish;

Red, rough sapotas;[7] red plums; yellow or vermillion plums; ashen sapotas;[8] small sapotas;[9] manioc;[10] sweet potato; avocado; yellow sapotas;[11] tuna cactus fruit of many hues—white, yellow, bright red, green, orange; anonas;[12] *guamúchiles;*[13] American cherries; tender maize;[14] green maize; string beans;

Tamales made of maize flowers with ground amaranth seed and cherries added; tortillas of green maize or of tender maize; tamales stuffed with amaranth greens;[15] tortillas made with honey, or with tuna cactus fruit; tamales made with honey; tortillas shaped like hip guards; tamales made of amaranth seed dough; [cakes made of] amaranth seed dough; rabbit with toasted maize; squash cut in pieces; *olchicalli;* green maize cooked in a pot and dried; amaranth greens cooked with dry land chili; sauce of purslain with dry land chili; green amaranth seeds with dry land chili;

Water greens; onions;[16] the evil-smelling herb; the *eloquilite* herb;[17] the *mozote* herb;[18] rabbit-ear greens; *achochoquilitl;*[19] thistle; sow thistle; sorrel of various kinds; a water-edge plant called *acuitlacpalli;* squash flowers; tender, young squash; small squash; garden cress; *raphanus;* small tuna cactus fruit with fish eggs;

tlatlauhquj teçontzapotl ixochiqual maçaxocotl chichiltic, coztic, tlaztaleoaltic, eheiotzapotl, xicotzapotl, quauhcamotli, camotli, aoacatl, atztzapotl, nochtli, tlatlatlapalpoalli, iztac, coztic, chichiltic, xoxoctic, camopaltic, matzatli, quammochil, capoli, xilotl, elotl, exotl,

mjiaoatamalli tlaixnamjctilli oauhtli ioan capoli, elotlaxcalli, anoço xantlaxcalli, xilotlaxcalli, oauhqujltamalli, necutlaxcalli, nochtlaxcalli, necutamalli, queçeoatlaxcalli, tzoallaxcalli, tzoalli, tochizqujtl, aiotlatlapanalli, olchicalli, elotl tlapaoaxtli tlaoatzalli, oauhqujlmolli tonalchillo, itzmjqujlmolli, tonalchillo, oauhtzontli tonalchillo,

tzaianalqujlitl, xonacatl, hijacaqujlitl, eloqujlitl, moçoqujlitl, nacaztochqujlitl, achochoqujlitl, ujtzqujlitl, chichicaquilitl, iztac xoxocoioli, xoxocoiolujujlan, axoxoco acujtlacpalli, aioxochqujlitl, aionanacatl, aioiacaqujlitl, aiotepitoton, mexixqujlitl, popoiauhqujlitl, nopaltepitoton mjchteuhio,

---

5. In Hernández, *op. cit.,* III, p. 746, this is *Porophyllum macrocephalum* DC.

6. Sahagún (*op. cit.,* III, p. 194) says of *topotli:* "*son pardillos críanse en los manantiales, son buenos de comer y sabrosos.*"

7. Hernández, *op. cit.,* I, p. 271: *Lucuma mammosa* Gaertn. Cf. also Santamaría, *op. cit.,* III, p. 314—"*tezonzapote o sapotecolorado que es el verdadero* ZAPOTE." Sahagún (*op. cit.,* III, p. 225) describes the *tecotzápotl* as "*de hechura y grandor del corazón de carnero; tienen la corteza áspera y tiesa, son colorados por de dentro, son muy dulces y muy buenos de comer, y tienen los cuescos negros muy lindos y relucientes.*" Cf. *teçonoa* in Molina, *op. cit.:* "*hazer aspera alguna cosa.*"

8. "*Son las anonas*" (Sahagún, *op. cit.,* p. 225); also corresponding Spanish text.

9. "*Llámanlos los españoles peruétanos* [wild or choke pear tree]. *Son muy dulces; hácense en tierra caliente*" (Sahagún, *op. cit.,* p. 224). In Hernández, *op. cit.,* I, p. 273, this is *Achras zapota* L.

10. *Ibid.,* II, p. 525: *Manihot esculenta* Crantz; Sahagún, *op. cit.,* p. 335: *guacamote* or *cazabe. Manihot utilissima* Pohl; in *ibid.,* p. 227, "*las raíces de estos árboles cuécense y hácense como batatas, y son de buen comer.*"

11. Hernández, *op. cit.,* I, p. 267 (*atzapotl*): *Lucuma salicifolia* Kunth; Sahagún, *op. cit.,* p. 224: "*son amarillos de dentro y de fuera; son muy dulces, tiesos a manera de yema de huevo cocida, tienen cuescos de color castaño oscuro.*"

12. *Anona squamosa, pomme cannelle,* in Siméon, *op. cit.;* Santamaría, *op. cit.,* II, p. 260: *Ananas sativus,* Schult.

13. Hernández, *op. cit.,* III, p. 799: *Pithecollobium dulce* (Roxb.) Benth.; cf. also Santamaría, *op. cit.,* II, p. 52 (*Guamúchil*).

14. Cf. Molina, *op. cit.* Santamaría, *op. cit.,* II, p. 149: "*Jilote: Cabellitos de la mazorca de maíz tierno.*"

15. Cf. Anderson and Dibble, *op. cit.,* I, p. 12; II, p. 154; esp. *ibid.,* I, p. 12, n. 66 (*uauhquilitl*).
See also Jonathan D. Sauer: "The Grain Amaranths: A Survey of Their History and Classification," *Annals of the Missouri Botanical Garden,* 37: 561-632 (Nov., 1950), where it is suggested that *uauhtli* may refer to either the chenopods or amaranths (p. 564).

16. *Allium* sp., in Sahagún, *op. cit.,* p. 339.

17. *Biddens pilosa* L.—*té de milpa* (Sahagún, *op. cit.,* p. 338). See also Santamaría, *op. cit.,* III, p. 337.

18. *Mozote* in Santamaría, *op. cit.,* II. p. 310. Sahagún, *op. cit.,* p. 338, has "*Yerba del Ángel,* Eupatorium deltoideaum. *Jacq. Compuestas*"; *quauheloquilitl* is the same.

19. Hernández, *op. cit.,* II, p. 361; *Bidens chrysanthemoides* Michx.; Sahagún, *op. cit.,* p. 338: *Bidens tetragona* D. C.

Gophers with sauce; hot maize gruel of many kinds; maize gruel with honey, with chili and honey, with yellow chili; white, thick gruel with a scattering of maize grains; sour, white maize gruel; sour, red maize gruel with fruit and chili; small, green tomatoes[20] with a maize gruel made with anonas; maize gruel made with amaranth and toasted maize; maize gruel with fish-amaranth seeds and honey; cold maize gruel; maize gruel with wrinkled chía,[21] covered with green chilis or small, hot chilis;[22] white maize gruel with chía,[23] covered with yellow chilis; maize gruel with chía, covered with squash seeds and with chili; maize gruel made of tortilla crumbs, and with ordinary and wrinkled chía, covered with small chilis.

All these foods came forth from within the house of the ruler.

And daily a man, the majordomo, set out for the ruler his food—two thousand kinds of various foods; hot tortillas, white tamales with beans forming a sea shell on top; red tamales; the main meal of roll-shaped tortillas and many [foods]: sauces with turkeys, quail, venison, rabbit, hare, gopher, lobster, small fish, large fish; then all [manner of] sweet fruits.

And when the ruler had eaten, then all the food was divided. Apart, in the city, the lords ate, and all the people from surrounding lands—the ambassadors, the war messengers, the princes, the judges, the high priests, the seasoned warriors, the valiant men of war, the masters of the youths, the rulers of the youths, the keepers of the gods, the priests, the singers, [the ruler's] pages, his servants, his jugglers, and the various artisans, goldsmiths, feather workers, cutters of precious stones, setters of mosaic, sandal makers, and turquoise cutters.[24]

Then, in his house, the ruler was served his chocolate, with which he finished [his repast]—green, made of tender cacao; honeyed chocolate made with ground-up dried flowers—with green vanilla pods; bright red chocolate; orange-colored chocolate; rose-colored chocolate; black chocolate; white chocolate.[25]

toçanmolli, totonquj atolli, mjiec tlamantli, nequatolli, chilnequatolli, chilcozio, quauhnexatolli tlatzincujtl, iztac xocoatolli, chichiltic, chilxocoatolli, mjltomatl inamjc eheioatolli, oauhatolli izqujo, mjchioaoatolli necuio, itztic atolli, chiantzotzolatolli, chilchopanj, anoço chiltecpinpanj, iztac chianatolli chilcozpanj, chianpitzaoac atolli, aiohoachpanj chillo, tlaçiocuepalatolli chiantzotzollo, ioan chianio chiltecpinpanj

in jxqujch tlamantli, y, tlaqualli icalitic, oalqujça tlatoanj.

Auh in momoztlae, ice tlacatl calpixquj qujtequjlia in tlatoanj, in jtlaqual macujltzontli in nepapan tlaqualli, in totonquj tlaxcalli in jztac quatecujcujlli in chichiltic tamalli, in vej tlaqualli, tlaxcalmjmjlli: ioan cenca mjiec tlamantli in jmollo in jvical in totoli, çolli, maçanacatl, tochi, çitli, tuçan, chacali, topotli, tlacamjchin, njman iee in jxqujch necutic xochiqualli.

Auh in jquac in otlaqua tlatoanj, njman ic moxexeloa, in jxqujch tlaqualli: nononqua tlaqua in altepetl ipan tlatoque, ioan in jxqujch cemanaoacatl in tlatocatitlanti, in moiautitlãque, in tlaçopipilti, in tecutlatoque, achcacauhti, tequjoaque, tiacahoan, tiachcahoan, telpuchtlatoque teupixque, tlamacazque, cujcanjme, in quezqujtlamantli, ixoloa, iiahachhoan, tetlaueuetzqujtique: ioan nepapan toltecatl, teucujtlapitzque, amanteca, tlatecque, chalchiuhtlacujloque, caççoque, teuxinque.

Niman moteca in jcalitic: iecauj in jcacaoauh, xoxouhquj cacaoaçintli, quauhnecujo cacaoatl, xochiocacaoatl, xoxouhquj tlilxochio, chichiltic cacaoatl, vitztecolcacaoatl, xochipalcacaoatl, tiltic cacaoatl, itztac cacaoatl

20. *Ibid.*, p. 237; small tomatoes; Siméon, *op. cit.*, green; Hernández, *op. cit.*, III, p. 699: "*los más chicos* miltomame, *es decir*, de siembra."

21. Sahagún, *op. cit.*, p. 364: "*Chía arrugada. Salvia ¿sp?*" Santamaría, *op. cit.*, III, p. 466: *Salvia polystachia*; Hernández, *op. cit.*, I, p. 210: *Salvia hispanica* Linn.

22. Santamaría, *op. cit.*, I, p. 496: *Capsicum microcarpum* Dc.—"*En Méjico, chile indígena, como del tamaño de una pulga y muy picante.*" In Hernández, *op. cit.*, II, p. 435, it is identified as *C. frutescens* L., *var. baccatum* L.: "*del nombre de los mosquitos, a los que parece imitar en la pequeñez y en el color.*"

23. Sahagún, *op. cit.*, p. 364: "*Salisa hispánica. L. Salides*"; Santamaría, *op. cit.*, I, p. 480: *Salvia chian, S. hispánica* L.

24. The Spanish text has barbers, which would require *texinque*.

25. *Tiltic* and *itztac* are as they appear in the Codex; *tliltic* and *iztac* are probably meant.

The chocolate was served in a painted gourd vessel, with a stopper also painted with a design, and [having] a beater; or in a painted gourd, smoky [in color], from neighboring lands, with a gourd stopper, and a jar rest of ocelot skin or of cured leather. In a small net were kept the earthen jars, the strainer with which was purified the chocolate, a large, earthen jar for making the chocolate, a large painted gourd vessel in which the hands were washed, richly designed drinking vessels; [there were] large food baskets, sauce dishes, polished dishes, and wooden dishes.

injc motecaia cacaoatl, tecontlacujlolli, atzaccaiotl tlacujlolli, aquaujtl aiotectli tlacujlolli, poctecomatl anaoacaiotl, atzaccaiotl aiotectli, aiaoalli oçeloeoatl, cuetlaxaiaoalli, chitatli in vncan mopia tecomatl, atzetzeloaztli, injc moiectia cacaoatl, vevei tecomatl achioalonj, vevej tlacujlolxicalli injc nematequjlo, tzohoacalli tlaioalonj, tlaqualchiqujujtl, molcaxitl, petzcaxitl, quauhcaxitl.

Fourteenth Chapter: here are described the palace and the houses of the lords: how were kept the houses of the lords [and] the great palace where the ruler dwelt; [how] all the lords[1] were disposed there, and there were determined the tributes or warfare; and in that place there was eating and drinking when the ruler assembled the people there.

FIRST PARAGRAPH, in which is described the court of justice, the high court, [in which], when something was harmed, when some did evil, there they passed judgment on them.

Tlacxitlan:[2] there were the rulers, the princes, and the high judges. All the complaints of the lower classes and common folk they there heard and judged. And all death [sentences] they there meted out; either they would strangle one with a cord, or stone him to death, or slay him under wooden staves,[3] beaten; or some nobleman or judge was to be shaven [as a disgrace], or driven [out of the land], or confined, or made a commoner; or one would be seized and jailed in a wooden cage.[4] And there they delivered slaves from [undeserved] bondage.

[When] Moctezuma was lord, there was famine for two years, and many noblemen sold their young sons and maidens. When Moctezuma heard of this, he commanded that all [these] noble youths be brought together, and that their masters be told that their goods [which they had paid for them] were to be restored and returned to them. With large capes and mantles, and dried maize grains he paid the price for the noblemen. And a double forfeit he then paid in order to redeem and deliver the noblemen from bondage.

In that place, the Tlacxitlan, they did not delay the hearings. At once, forthwith, a judgment was pro-

Injc 14. capitulo vncan mjtoa in tecpancalli in tlatocacalli, ic mopia tlatocacalli, vej tecpan in vncan ca tlatoanj, ixqujch tlacatl vncan tecpanoa, vncan motzontequj in tlein tequjtl, anoçe iauiotl: ioan vncan atlioa tlaqualo, injc vnca tecenqujxtia tlatoanj.

INJC CE PARRAPHO ipan mjtoa in vncã tlatoloia, in audiençia in jquac itla itlacauija, in aqujque tlatlacoa, vncan qujntlatzontequjliaia.

Tlacxitlan, vncan catca tlatoque tlaçopipilti, tecutlatoque: in jxqujch tlamantli in jneteilhujl cujtlapilli atlapalli maçeoalli: vnca qujcaqujliaia, vncan qujtlatzontequjliaia; ioan ixqujch tlamantli mjqujztli vncan qujtzontequja aço aca quimecanjzque, anoço aca qujtetepachozque, anoço aca quauhtica mjqujz qujujujtequjzque, anoço aca pilli, anoço tecutlato, ximaloz, totocoz, callaliloz, maceoalcuepaloz, anoço aca ilpiloz quauhcalco tlaliloz: ioan vncan qujntlatlacollaçaia, in tlatlacoti.

Tlatocati in motecuçuma, oxiujtl in maianaloc, in pipilti mjiequjntin, in qujnnamacaque in jntelpuchoan, ioan in jmjchpuchoan, in jcoac in oqujcac motecuçuma: tlanaoati injc nechicolozque, in jxqujchtin tlaçotipipilti, ioan notzalozque in jntecujiohoan, injc macozque, injc cuepililozque in jntlatquj. Veuej tilmatli, ioan quachtli, ioan tlaolli, injc qujmpatiotica pipilti, ioã oppamjxtlapan injc qujntlaxtlaujli, injc qujntlatlacollaz pipilti.

In oncan jn tlacxitlan amo tle vecaoaia in neteilhujlli, çan njman iciuhca motzontequja, in tlein

1. Cf. Sahagún, op. cit., III, pp. 22-23: "Este nombre, tlácatl, quiere decir, persona noble, generosa o magnífica. . . . Y los compuestos de tlácatl que se componen con nombres numerales, significan persona común, como diciendo ce tlácatl, una persona hombre, o mujer." Also cf. Leonhard Schultze Jena: Gliederung des Alt-Aztekischen Volks in Familie, Stand und Beruf, aus dem Aztekischen Urtext Bernardino de Sahagun's (Stuttgart: W. Kohlhammer Verlag, 1952), p. 32.
2. Clark, op. cit., I, p. 97, defines the term as the highest criminal court, meaning "those placed below, at the feet."
3. See Pl. 66.
4. See Pls. 67, 87.

nounced. And in what was there made known, the lords did nothing for friendship's sake; they exacted nothing as reward; nor delayed [any case].

SECOND PARAGRAPH, which telleth of the court, the place of discussion, where spoke the judges.

Teccalli,[5] or Teccalco: there were the judges and noblemen.[6] Every day the common folk and vassals laid complaints before them. Calmly and prudently they heard the plaints of the vassals; in the picture writing which recorded the case, they studied the complaints. And when they tested their truth, they sought out and inquired of informers and witnesses who could size up the plaintiffs, [who knew] what had been stolen and what was charged.

And the ruler, if he knew anything ill of these judges—perhaps that they needlessly delayed the case of common folk, that they deliberated two years or even four—[that] they could not pronounce judgment because of either a bribe or kinship,—he then seized them and jailed them in wooden cages, exacted the penalty, and slew them, so that the judges might walk in dread.

[When] Moctezuma was lord, he learned many ill things of the judges Mixcoatlailotlac, Teicnotlamachti, Tlacochcalcatl, Iztlaca mixcoatlailotlac, Umaca, Toqual, Uictlolinqui, [all] of Tlatilulco—that they had unjustly discharged their office of judge. Then he seized them, jailed them in wooden cages, exacted the penalty, and slew them.

THIRD PARAGRAPH, in which is described the place of discussion where were the brave warriors and the noblemen.

Tecpilcalli: there were [to be found] and were established the noblemen, the brave warriors,[7] the valiant men, wise in war. If the ruler knew something ill of some nobleman—although he were a great prince,[8] or brave warrior—if he had committed adultery, then he sentenced him to be stoned before the people, to die stoned.

[When] Moctezuma was lord, one who was a prince, named Uitznauatl ecamalacotl, committed

vncan caqujtiloia tlatoque atle qujcnjuhchioaia atle tlaxtlaujltica qujxpachoaia, anoço qujuecaoaia.

INJC VME PARRAPHO, itechpa tlatoa in audiençia in tlatoloian in vncan tlatoaia tecutlatoque.

Teccalli, teccalco, vncan catca in tecutlatoque, in tetecuti, in momuztlae imjxpan moteilhujaia, cujtlapilli atlapalli maçeoalli, iujian iocuxca, in qujcaquja in jnneteilhujl maçeoalli: tlapallacujlolpan in qujpoaia, in qujttaia neteilhujlli: auh injc qujnneltiliaia, qujntemoaia, qujmjtlanja in machiceque, in tlaneltilianj, in qujmachilia moteilhujque, in tlein qujmocujcujlia, in tlein ipan moteilhuja.

Auh in tlatoanj, intla itla qujnmachili in iehoantin tecutlatoque, aço çã tlapic qujuecaoa, in jneteilhujl cujtlapilli, atlapalli, aço ie uxiujtl, anoço ie nauhxiujtl qujnemjtia in amo uel qujtzontequj, aço çan ipampa tlaxtlaujlli, anoço hoaiolcaiotl: njman qujmjlpia, quauhcalco qujntlalia, qujtzacutiuj, qujmjctia, injc mauhca iezque tecutlatoque.

Tlatocati motecuçuma, mjiec tlamantli in qujnmachili tecutlatoque mjxcoatlailotlac teicnotlamachti, tlacochcalcatl, iztlaca mjxcoatlailotlac vmaca, toqual, victlolinquj, tlatilulco in amo melaoac qujchioaia in jntequjuh tecutlatolli: njman qujmjlpi, quauhcalco qujntlali, qujtzacutiaque, qujnmjcti.

INJC EI PARRAPHO: vncan mjtoa in tlatoloian, in vncan catca in tiacaoan, ioan in pipilti.

Tecpilcalli, vncan catca, vncan tecpanoaia in pipilti, tiacahoan oqujchti, in iauc matinj, in tlatoanj intla aca itla qujmachili pilli, in manel cenca tlaçopilli tiacauh intla otetlaxin, njman qujtlatzontequjlia, injc teixpan tetepacholo tetica mjquj

motecuçuma tlatocati, ce tlacatl tlaçopilli itoca vitznaoatl ecamalacotl tetlaxi in oconteixpauique ix-

---

5. Sahagún, in the corresponding Spanish text, refers to all of these places as "another hall"—"otra sala."

6. Manuel Orozco y Berra, in Historia antigua y de la conquista de México (México: Tipografía de Gonzalo A. Esteva, 1880), I, p. 267, explains that "En cada barrio de México había un teuctli, electo anualmente por los vecinos; determinaba de causas livianas, dando cuenta diariamente á los jueces superiores." Clark, (op. cit., I, p. 97) writes: "The four seated figures behind the judges, called tectli, are young men of rank who attend the courts for instruction, so that in time they might rise to the position of judge." (See also ff. 67v and 68r of the Mendoza Codex.)

7. Tiacauh, pilli, tecpilli: cf. Sahagún, op. cit., III, p. 26; Jena, op. cit., pp. 34, 68.

8. Tlaçopilli: cf. Jena, op. cit., p. 34.

adultery. They accused him before Moctezuma, who then condemned him to be stoned before the people.

FOURTH PARAGRAPH, in which is discussed the council chamber of the brave warriors devoted to war.

Tequiuacacalli or Quauhcalli: there were the brave warriors, the generals, and the commanding generals,[9] whose personal charge was command in war.

Achcauhcalli: there were the constables, the brave warriors who were the ruler's executioners. These who brought to an end [the life of] any upon whom sentence had fallen [were] the Quauhnochtli, Atempanecatl, and Tezcacoacatl. And if they erred in something, they exacted the penalty of them and they died.

Cuicacalli: there were the masters of the youths and the rulers of the youths, there established in order to oversee what was by way of work. And every day, when the sun had already set, they turned their attention to dances. They went quite naked. So they went to the house of songs; so they danced with song, proceeding with, about their necks, only [a cape] made like a net. They set in place and proceeded with their forked heron feather ornaments and the red cord with which they bound their hair; and [they had] their turquoise ear plugs and sea shell lip pendants. All the youths, when they danced and sang, ceased when it was well into the night, when for the first time the fire priests and [other] priests blew the shell trumpets. None of [the youths] entered their homes; none slept at home. Rather, they went straight to the young men's houses, which were everywhere. There they slept, stretched out quite naked. Only little did they sleep. On the morrow, when it was still dark, they set forth, to lodge in the house of the ruler.

And when the ruler knew something ill of them—either drunkenness or concubinage;[10] or that they wrought something to their advantage behind the back of the ruler; [or] that without his command they levied tribute on the town, perchance of chocolate, or of food, which became a tribute, and it was done without leave, and [that] they exacted as tribute whatsoever they wished, then the ruler commanded that they be jailed in wooden cages. He condemned them to pay the penalty; perchance they strangled

pan motecuçuma, njman qujoallatzontequjli, injc teixpan tetepacholoc.

IC NAUJ PARRAPHO, vncan mjtoa in jnnenonotzaia in tiacahoan in jpampa iaujotl.

Tequjoacacalli, quauhcalli, vncan catca in tiacaoan tlacochcalcatl tlacatecatl, in jnneixcaujl iautequj:

Achcauhcalli vncan catca in achcacauhti in tiacahoan in jtemjcticaoan catca tlatoanj, iehoantin qujtzonqujxtiaia in aqujn tlein ipan omotzontec, quauhnochtli, atempanecatl, tezcacoacatl, auh in jtla qujtlacoaia, qujtzacutiuja mjquja.

Cujcacalli, vncan catca in tiachcahoan, in telpuchtlatoque vncan tlatecpanoaia injc qujchiaia tlein tequjtl, auh in momuztlae, in jquac ie calaquj tonatiuh: tlamaçeoaliztli ipan qujmatia, çan petlauhtiuja, injc viia cujcacali, injc oncujcoanooaia çanijo inquech in onactiuja, iuhqujn matlatl ic tlachiuhtli, imaztaxel conmantiuj, tochacatl injc qujlpia intzonchichilicpatl: ioan ixiuhnacoch, ioan intempilol eptli, ixqujch in telpuchtli in oncujcoanoia icoac necaoaloia in tlaquauhtlapoiaoa, in jcoac iancujcan tlapitzaia tlenamacaque tlamacazque, amo ac ichan calaquja, amo ac ichan oncochia, ca njman vmpa tlamelaoaia, in noujian telpuchcalli mamanca: in oncan cochia, çan pepetlauhtoca, çan achi in concochia, momoztlae in oc iohoan qujça in ontecpanoa, yn ichan tlatoanj.

Auh in jcoac itla qujnmachilia in tlatoanj, aço tlaoanaliztli, anoço nemecatiliztli, anoço itla icampa qujqujxtia, in tlatoanj: in amo itencopa, itla qujtetequjtia in calla aço atl, tlaqualli tequjpan iecauj, moiocoia, qujtetequjtia injc intech monequj, njman tlanaoatia in tlatoanj, quauhcalco qujntlalia, qujntlatzontequjlia, injc qujtzacutiuj, aço qujnmecanja, anoço qujntetepachoa, anoço quauhtica qujnujujtequj teixpan, injc mjctilo, injc maujztli qujteca tlatoanj.

---

9. *Tlacochcalcatl, tlacatecatl*: see Sahagún, *op. cit.*, III, p. 27; Jena, *op. cit.*, p. 70; Anderson and Dibble, *op. cit.*, II, p. 102, n. 3; III, pp. 57-58.
10. After *nemecatiliztli*, the *Real Academia de la Historia MS* has *anoço tetlaximaliztli*—or adultery.

them with a cord, or they stoned them, or before the people they beat them with wooden [staves], so that they were slain. Thus the ruler implanted fear.[11]

FIFTH PARAGRAPH, where is told how they stored all the food.

Petlacalco: there was stored all the food. Dried maize grains thus were kept in wooden grain bins; more than two thousand [measures of] grains of dried maize—a store of twenty years for the city. And in wooden storage bins were dried beans, chía, amaranth seeds, wrinkled chía, salt jars, coarse salt, baskets of chilis, baskets of squash seeds, and large squash seeds. And there was kept the jail, the wooden cage,[12] where they imprisoned and confined evildoers.

SIXTH PARAGRAPH, in which is described the house of the majordomos and stewards.

Calpixcalli[13] or Texancalli: there assembled all the majordomos and tribute gatherers. There they were lodged [to await the command of the ruler, (lest) he require something, or] to bring down and put in order that which was their trust as tributes, [and there they arranged in order the various foods] which every day they gave the ruler. And if the ruler knew something ill of a majordomo, perchance of something he stole from the tributes; or that all his charge, the tributes, perhaps did not equal the correct count when all his store was tallied and examined; then he jailed the majordomo in a wooden cage; he exacted the penalty, that he die. Then he cast out his women [and his children from his home]. Then quickly the house of the majordomo was closed up, and all his goods remained in the house. All belonged to the ruler.

Coacalli: there were established all the lords from everywhere—friends of the ruler, and all the lords unfriendly to him. He gave and bestowed upon them all manner of costly goods: valuable capes and breech clouts, golden lip plugs, golden ear plugs, green stone lip plugs, green stone necklaces, and green stone bracelets.

IC MACUJLLI PARRAPHO: vncan mjtoa injc qujpiaia in jxqujch qualonj.

Petlacalco, vncan mopiaia, in jxqujch qualonj, in tlaolli, injc mopiaia quauhquezcomatl, amo çan macujltzontli, vncatca tlaolli: cempoalxiuhcaiotl, in jtetzon altepetl, ioan quauhcuezcontica mamanca in etl, in chian, in oauhtli, in chiantzotzol, iztacomjtl, iztaxalli, chilpetlatl, aiooachpetlatl, quauhaiooachtli: ioan vncan mopiaia in teilpilcalli, quauhcalli, in vncan qujmjlpiaia, qujncaltzaquaia tlatlacoanj.

IC CHIQUACEN PARRAPHO, vncã mjtoa: in jnchan mayordomos in calpixque.

Calpixcalli, texancalli, vncã cenqujçaia: in jxqujch calpixquj, ioan tequjtquj, vncan tecpanoaia injc [quitlatolchixticatca tlatoani, aço tlein quinequiz, aço] tlein qujtemoz qujcencauhticatca, in tlein inpiel tlacalaqujlli, [yoan uncan quicenquixtiaya y nepapan tlaqualli,] in momoztlae qujmacaia tlatoanj. Auh intla tlatoanj, itla qujmachili, ce calpixquj, aço itla qujnaoalchioa tlacalaqujlli: ioan in jxqujch in jpiel, in tlacalaqujlli: acaçomo caçi in tlapoaliztli: in jcoac mopoa, mocxitoca, in jxqujch in jpiel; njman quauhcalco qujtlalia, in calpixquj: qujtzacutiuh, mjquj, njman qujnqujxtia, in jçioahoan [yoan in ipilhoan yn ichan]: njman içiuhca motzaqua, in jcal calpixquj ioan in jxqujch in jtlatquj, calitic onoc: moch itech compoã tlatoanj.

Coacalli vncan tecpanoaia, in jxqujchtin, noujian tlatoque: in jicnjhoan tlatoanj, ioan in jxqujchtin, iiauhoan tlatoque: qujnmacaia, qujntlauhtiaia, in jxqujch tlaçotli, in tlaçotilmatli, in tlaçomaxtlatl, in teucujtlatentetl, in teucujtlanacochtli, in chalchiuhtentetl, in chalchiuhcozcatl, in chalchiuhmacuextli.

11. At the end of this paragraph, the *Real Academia de la Historia* MS contains an account of the Calmecac, which is lacking in the *Florentine Codex*. (See Appendix A.)

12. *Teilpilcalli, quauhcalli:* Orozco y Berra, *op. cit.*, I, pp. 268-269, writes: "*Las prisiones eran de dos especies. La llamada teilpiloyan, lugar de presos, en que estaban detenidos los delincuentes de penas leves; el cuauhcalli, casa de madera, especie de jaula fuerte de vigas, en que se guardaba los condenados á la muerte y prisioneros de guerra destinados al sacrificio.*"

13. In the *Real Academia de la Historia* MS, three passages appear which are not in the *Florentine Codex*. Because they change the sense to a degree, they are here inserted in brackets.

SEVENTH PARAGRAPH, in which is told how the singers bedizened themselves when the ruler would dance; and of that in which they would dance.

Mixcoacalli: there were established all the kinds of singer-dancers of Tenochtitlan and Tlatilulco. There they awaited the word of the ruler, that he would dance, or try some song, or learn some new song. All this the singers prepared, all that was necessary—two-toned drums, rubber drum hammers, ground drums, gourd rattles, copper bells, flutes; players of two-toned drums and ground drums, intoners of chants, leaders of the dance; and all the properties used in the dance.

If the song were to be intoned after the manner of Uexotzinco, they were adorned like men of Uexotzinco, and spoke even as they did; they were imitated with the song and in their adornment and their equipment. Likewise if a song were to be intoned after the manner of Anauac, the speech of the men of Anauac was imitated, and their adornment as well as their equipment. Likewise, if a song were to be intoned after the manner of the Huaxteca, their speech was imitated, and their headdresses were taken, with which to imitate them in coloring their hair yellow; and the masks [had] arrow marks [painted] on the face, noses pierced like jug handles, teeth filed [to a point], and conical heads. And they [were clad] only in their capes. Likewise [they did] other songs.

EIGHTH PARAGRAPH, which telleth of the houses in which were the slaves.

Malcalli: the majordomos guarded[13a] the captives. They took great care of them as to food and drink. That which they needed, they gave all to the captives.

Totocalli: there majordomos kept all the various birds—eagles, red spoonbills, trupials, yellow parrots, parakeets, large parrots, pheasants. And there all the various artisans did their work: the gold and silversmiths, the copper-smiths, the feather workers,[14] painters, cutters of stones, workers in green stone mosaic, carvers of wood. Caretakers of wild animals,[15] majordomos, there guarded all the wild animals: ocelots, bears, mountain lions, and mountain cats.

INJC CHICOME PARRAPHO, vncã mjtoa, injc mocencaoaia cujcanjme, in tlamaceoaz tlatoanj: ioan in tlein ipan mjtotizque.

Mixcoacalli, vncan tecpanoaia in jzqujtlamantli, mâcehoalcujcanjme in tenochca, ioan tlatilulcatl, vncan qujtlatolchiaia in tlatoanj, in aço mâçeoaz, aço itla cujcatl qujiehecoz, aço itla iancujc cujcatl qujmomachtiz, mochi ic moçencauhticatca, in cujcanjme: in jxqujch monequj teponaztli, olmaitl, veuetl, aiacachtli, tetzilacatl, çoçoloctli, teponaçoanj, veuetzonanj, cujcaitoanj teiacanque: ioan in ixqujch tlamantli mâcehoallatqujtl,

intla uexotzincaiotl meoaz cujcatl, in iuh muchichioa vexotzinca, ioan in iuh tlatoa: motlaiehecalhuja in jca cujcatl: ioan ica inechichioal intlaquj. Çan no iuhquj intla anaoacaiotl meoaz, motlaiehecalhuja, in jntlatol anaoaca: ioan jnnechichioal in iuhquj intlatquj. Çan no iuhquj, intla cuextecaiotl meoaz cujcatl, motlaiehecalhuja in jntlatol: ioan mocuj tzoncalli in qujntlaiehecalhuja, intzon, injc quacoztique, ioan xaiacatl ixtlamjoa iacaujcole, tlantziquatic, quapatlachtic, içan jtilma. Can no iuhquj in oc cequj cujcatl.

INJC CHICUEJ PARRAPHO, ipan tlatoa, in jnchan catca tlatlacoti

Malcalli: calpixque pinpiaia, in mamalti, cenca qujnmocujtlaujaia, in tlaqualtica, in atica: in tlein qujnequja, mochi qujnmacaia in mamalti.

Totocalli, calpixque vncan qujnpiaia, in jxqujch nepapan tototl: quaquauhti, tlauhquechol, çaquan, tozneneme, cochome, alome, coxoliti: ioan oncan tlachichioaia, in jxqujch nepapan toltecatl, in teucujtlapitzquj, in tepozpitzquj, in amanteca, tlacujloque, tlatecque, chalchiuhtlacujloque, quauhtlacujloque Tequanpixque, calpixque, vncan qujnpiaia, in jxqujch tequanj: oçelotl, cuetlachtli, mjztli, ocotochtli.

13a. *Pinpiaia*: probably *quinpiaia* is meant.

14. "Feather-workers were called amanteca after the district of Amantlan, in Tenochtitlan, where they lived" (Clark, *op. cit.*, I, p. 56, n. 2). Cf. also Seler, *Einige Kapitel*, p. 378.

15. The *Real Academia de la Historia MS* has *tequanpixca* for *tequanpixque*, and begins with the term a new paragraph. A marginal gloss by Sahagún heads the section, *"Casa de las fieras."*

Fifteenth Chapter, in which is described the adornment of the women.

The orange colored shift gathered at the waist; the shift [decorated with] yellow parrot feathers; the shift with the stamp device at the neck; the shift with flowers overspread; the shift of smoky color; [shifts] with large embroidered [figures] at the throat, with [designs] of cut reeds; the shift with feathers; the tawny colored shift; the shift of coyote fur; the duck feather shift; [the shift] with dyed rabbit fur; the shift with the gourd and thistle [design]; the shift overspread with dahlias;[1] [the shift] with the eagle head in a setting, done in feathers; the shift with a border of flowers;

The skirt with an irregular [design], having a wide border; the skirt with serpent skins, having a wide border; the skirt with the step meander, having a wide border, the skirt with squared corner stones, having a wide border; the skirt with thin, black lines, having a wide border; the white skirt [like a] bed covering, having a wide border; the ocelot skin skirt, having a wide border; the skirt with brown pendants, having a border; the skirt with coyote fur pendants, having a border;

Amber ear plugs; white crystal ear plugs; golden ear plugs; silver ear plugs; white obsidian ear plugs.

Their faces were painted with dry, colored [powders]; faces were colored with yellow ochre, or with bitumen. Feet were anointed with an unguent of burned copal incense and dye. They had hair hanging to the waist, or to the shoulders; or the young girls' lock of hair; or the hair [twisted with black cord and] wound about the head; or the hair all cut the same length. [Some] cut their hair short, [so that] their hair reached to their noses.[2] It was cut and dyed with black mud—[so] did they place impor-

Ic caxtolli capitulo: vncan mjtoa in jnnechichioaia in çioa.

Vitztecolcujtlalpic vipilli, xoxoloio ujpilli, quechnenecujlhoazio vipilli, xuchimoiaoac ujpilli, pocujpilli, veuej tlamachtli itozquj, toltzaianquj, potoncaio vipilli, quappachio vipilli, coioichcaio vipilli, xomoiujvipilli, tlapaltochomjtica xicalnetzollo vipilli, acocoxuchimoiaoac vipilli, ixquauhcallo potoncaio xoxochiteio vipilli.

Chicocuejtl, patlaoac in jten: coatlaxipeoallo cueitl, patlaoac in jten, xicalcoliuhquj cueitl, patlaoac in jten, tetenacazio cuejtl, patlaoac in jten, tlilpipitzaoac cueitl, patlaoac in jten: cacamoliuhquj iztac cueitl, patlaoac in jten, oçelocuejtl, patlaoac in jtẽ; quappachpipilcac cuejtl, tene: coioichcapipilcac cuejtl tene.

Apoçonalnacochtli, teujlonacochtli iztac, coztic teucujtlanacochtlj: iztac teucujtlanacochtli, itznacochtli iztac.

Moxaoaia, tlapalhoatzaltica: moxaoaia, tecuçauhtica: mochapopoxaoaia: copalaxtica mocxioxiuja, tzonqueme, quatequeque, atzotzocoleque, maxtlaoa, motzonquetzaltia, qujquatequj in jntzon, qujiaiacanepanoa in jntzon: tlatetecoa, mopatinemj, qujmamaujizmati in jntzontecon: moxiuhqujlpa, injc pepetlaca intzon: motlantlapalhujia, motlãnochezuja, momaicujloa, moquechicujloa, moquechtetema, melchiqujuhicujloa, mochichioaticujloa.

---

1. In Hernández, *op. cit.*, I, p. 24, acocoxóchitl is identified as *Dahlia coccinea*, Cav. Santamaría (*op. cit.*, I, p. 35), however, says of acocote: "*En Méjico, variedad de calabaza común, indígena del país, conocida también por* alacate. (Lagenaria vulgaris, var.)." Manuel Urbina, in "Plantas comestibles de los antiguos mexicanos," *Anales* del Museo Nacional de México, segunda época, Tomo I, pp. 515*sqq.*, 519, mentions two kinds of acocoquilitl (acocotli, quilitl), of one of which Hernández is quoted to the effect that it has "*flores estrelladas purpúreas*"; Dr. Oliva is cited (Secc. de Farmacología, II, p. 276), giving *Pentascripta atropurpurea* D. C. for acocote; Urbina thinks it is *Arracacia atropurpurea* Benth et Hook.

2. After *in jntzon*, the *Real Academia de la Historia MS* has *mixquatecpiltia*—they left a tuft of hair over the forehead.

tance upon their heads; it was dyed with indigo,[3] so that their hair shone. The teeth were stained with cochineal; the hands and neck were painted with designs—the necks were covered [with painting]. The stomach and breasts were [also] painted with designs.

They bathed in the sweat house and with [soap and] water. They were held in esteem. They were modest, good, and of noble [mien]. Thus did they speak—attentively, and respectfully of others; they were diligent and considerate.

Motema, mahaltia, momamauizmati: pinaoanj, qualli maujztic, injc tlatoa: temauhcaittanj, teimacaçinj, hiçiuhcaioque, moiolitlacoanj.

---

3. *Xiuhquilitl*: Urbina (*op. cit.*, p. 566) mentions two kinds: *xiuhquilitl pitzahoac, Indigofera añil* Linn., and *xiuhquilitl patlahoac, Calliandra gracilis* Klotzsch—both producing a blue dye.

Sixteenth Chapter, in which it is told how the women were trained.

[Theirs were] the device with which [the loom] was held; the divided cord; the skein; the heddle; the cane stalks; the wide batten, which swished [as it was used]; the thin batten, one made of bone; the small batten with which they worked designs; the thick straws; the flail; the spindle whorl; the spinning bowl; chalk; the shallow spindle whorl when they spun with feathers; the basket for unspun cotton, one for rabbit hair, one for cotton thread, the basket for feathers, and the earthen bowl for feathers; the rack for yarn; the colored wood[1] with which they dyed cotton when they wove; the bowl for colors in which they dissolved pigments; the paper patterns from which they took the shape of whatsoever they made; maguey spines, with which they picked the cotton threads.

They took personal charge of preparing food and chocolate. There were their older women, who had reared them; and their hand-maidens were hunchbacks and dwarfs, who sang and played the [small ground] drum to amuse them.

Injc caxtolli oce capitulo, vncan mjtoa, injc moiehecoaia çioa.

Neanonj, mecamaxalli, quatzontli, xiiotl, otlatl, tzotzopaztli cacalaca, patlaoac: tzotzopaztli pitzaoac, omjtzotzopaztli, tzotzopaztepiton, ic tlamachioa: teçacatl, tlaujteconj, malacatl, tzaoalcaxitl, tiçatl, xaxalmalacatl ic iujtzaoa: ichcatanatli, tochomjtanatli, icpatanatli, iujtanatlj, iujtecomatl: tzatzaztli, tlacujlolquaujtl injc qujcujloa icpatl in qujqujti: tlapalcaxitl, in vncan qujpatla intlapal: amamachiotl, in vncan cana tlein tlamachtli qujchioa; vitztli injc qujuitzcuj icpatl:

tlaqualchioa, achioa, qujnomauja: vncate in jnnahoan in qujmjzcaltia, ioan in cocoa tepotzome çihoa, tzapame, cujca, tlatzotzona: injc melelqujxtia.

---

1. *Tlacujlolquaujtl:* Sahagún (*op. cit.,* III, p. 222) describes the trees as *"bermejos, y tienen las vetas negras que parecen pinturas sobre el bermejo; es árbol muy preciado, porque de él se hacen* teponaztles. *tamboriles y vihuelas. . . ."* One is pictured in Emmart, *op. cit.,* Pl. 69.

Seventeenth Chapter, in which are told the exercises of the rulers and how they might perform well their office and their government.

FIRST PARAGRAPH, where is told, as well, the ordering of those sent when war was waged.

The ruler was known as the lord of men. His charge was war. Hence, he determined, disposed, and arranged how war would be made.

First he commanded masters of the youths and seasoned warriors to scan the [enemy] city and to study all the roads—where [they were] difficult, where entry could be made through them. This done, the ruler first determined, by means of a painted [plan], how was placed the city which they were to destroy. Then the ruler noted all the roads —where [they were] difficult, and in what places entry could be made.

Then he summoned the general and the commanding general, and the brave warriors, and he commanded them how they were to take the road, what places the warriors were to enter, for how many days they would march, and how they would arrange the battle. And he commanded that these would announce war and send forth all the men dexterous in war to be arrayed, and to be supplied with provisions for war and insignia.

The ruler then consulted with all the majordomos —the men of the Petlacalli[1] and of the Aztacalli, the majordomos of Quauhnauac and Uaxtepec, and [those] of Cuetlaxtlan, Tochpan, Tziuhcoac, Tepequacuilco, Uapan, Coatlixtlauacan, Tlappan, Tlachco, Matlatzinco, Ocuillan, Xilotepec, Atotonilco, Axocopan, Itzcuincuitlapilco, Atocpan, and Ayotzintepec. He ordered them to take out all their [goods held in] storage, the tributes, costly articles—insignia of gold, and with quetzal feathers, and all the shields of great price.

And when the majordomos had delivered all the costly devices, the ruler then adorned and presented with insignia all the princes who were already able in war, and all the brave warriors, the men [at arms],

Injc caxtolli omome cap°, vncan mjtoa in jnneiehecoliz in tlatoque: in quenjn vel qujchioazque intequjuh, in jntlatocaio.

INJC CE PARRAPHO: vncan mjtoa, ioan in tlatecpanaliztli, in qujtitlanja injc iauuqujçaia.

In tlatoanj, tlacatecutli, motocaiotia: itequjuh catca in iauiotl, injc iehoatl qujtzontequj, qujtecpana, qujçencahoa, in quenjn mochioaz iauiotl:

achto qujnaoatia in tiachcahoan, in tequjoaque, in connemjlia altepetl, in conjtta, in quezquj vtli, in campa oujca, in campa ic calacoaz, in ie iuhquj achto oqujnemjli in tlatoanj, tlapallacujlolpan omotlali in altepetl, in poliujz, ie onjtztica in tlatoanj in izqui vtli, in campa oujcan, quezqujcan in calacoaz.

Niman ic qujoalnotza: in tlacuchcalcatl, in tlacateccatl, in tiacahoan qujnnaoatia, in iuh teumacazque in quezqujcan calaqujz iauuqujzquj, in quezqujlhujtl monenemiz, in quenjn iautecoz: ioan qujnnaoatia, injc iehoantin, iautlatozque qujnnaoatizque: in jxqujch in quauhtloçelotl, injc mochichioaz, injc moçencaoaz: in jca iauitacatl, ioã tlaujztli.

Auh in iehoatl tlatoanj: njman qujnnonotza in jxqujchtin calpixque, petlacalcatl, aztacalcatl: quauhnaoac calpixquj, oaxtepec calpixquj, cuetlaxtecatl: tochpanecatl: tziuhcoacatl, tepequacujlcatl, hoappanecatl, coaixtlaoacatl, tlappanecatl, tlachcotecatl, matlatzincatl, ocujltecatl, xilotepecatl, atotonjlcatl, axocopanecatl, itzcujncujtlapilcatl, atocpanecatl, aiotzintepecatl, qujnnaoatia, injc qujoalcujzque, in jxqujch in jnpiel, in tlacalaqujlli, in tlaçotlanquj tlaujztli in coztic teucujtlaio, in quetzallo: in jxqujch tlaçochimalli.

Auh in jcoac oqujoalitqujque in calpixque: in jxqujch tlaçotlanquj tlaujztli: iiehoatl tlatoanj, njman qujcencaoa qujntlaujzmaca in jxqujchtin tlaçopipilti, in ie imjxco ca iautiliztli: ioan in jxqujchtin

---

1. Cf. Anderson and Dibble, *op. cit.,* II, p. 99; Sahagún, *op. cit.,* I, p. 166; II, p. 311.

the seasoned warriors, the shorn ones, the Otomí, and the noblemen who dwelt in the young men's houses.

And when it had come to pass that the ruler adorned them, when he had done this to the brave warriors, then the ruler ordered all the majordomos to bear their goods, all the costly devices, and all the valuable capes there to battle, that the ruler might offer and endow with favors all the [other] rulers, and the noblemen, and the brave warriors, the men [at arms] who were about to go to war, who were to be extended as if made into a wall of men dexterous with arms. And the ruler forthwith called upon the rulers of Texcoco and Tlacopan and the rulers in all the swamp lands, and notified them to proclaim war in order to destroy a [certain] city. He presented them all with costly capes, and he gave them all insignia of great price. Then he also ordered the common folk[2] to rise to go forth to war. Before them would go marching the brave warriors, the men [at arms], the lord general, and the commanding general.

The lords of the sun, it was said, took charge and directed in war. All the priests, the keepers of the gods, took the lead; they bore their gods upon their backs, and, by the space of one day, marched ahead of all the brave warriors and the seasoned warriors. These also marched one day ahead of all the warriors of Tenochtitlan. Again these marched one day ahead of all the warriors of Tlatilulco. These also marched one day ahead of all the men of Acolhuacan, who likewise marched one day ahead of all the Tepaneca, who similarly marched one day ahead of the men of Xilotepec; and these also marched one day ahead of all the so-called Quaquata. In like manner the [men of] other cities were disposed. They followed the road slowly and carefully.

And when the warlike lands[3] were reached, the brave warrior generals and commanding generals then showed the others the way and arranged them in order. No one might break ranks or crowd in among the others; they would then and there slay or beat whoever would bring confusion or crowd in among the others. All the warriors were extended there, until the moment that Yacauitztli, [god of] the night, would descend—that darkness would fall.

tiacahoan, in oqujchtin, in tequjoaque, in quaquach-icti, in otomj: ioan in telpuchnemj in pipilti.

auh in ie iuhquj, in otecencauh tlatoanj, in tiacauh, in iuh oqujchiuh. Niman qujnnaoatia, in tlatoanj: in jxqujchtin calpixque, injc intlatquj ietiaz; in jx-qujch tlaçotlanquj, tlaujztli: ioan in jxqujch tlaçotil-matli, in vmpa iauc, in qujnmacaz, in qujntlauhtiz, in tlatoanj: In jxqujchtin tlatoque, ioan in pipilti, ioan in tiacahoan, in oqujchtin in iauteoatoque, in iuhquj oçelotenanti, quauhtenanti mochiuhtoque: ioan in tlatoanj, achto qujnnotza in tlatoanj tetzcuco, ioan tlacopan: ioan in jxqujch chinanpanecatl in tlatoque, qujncaqujtia, injc iautlatoa, injc poliujz ce altepetl: qujntlauhtia, in jxqujch tlaçotilmatli, ioan qujnmaca, in jxqujch tlaçotlanquj tlaujztli. Niman no ic qujnnaoatia: in jxqujch in jmaçeoal, injc iauqujçatiuh: impan hicatiuh in tiacaoan, in oqujch-tin, in tlacochcalcatl tecutli, ioan tlacateccatl,

tonatiuh itlatocahoan mjtoaia, qujiacana in qujujca iauc, iacattiuj in ixqujchtin tlamacazque, in teupix-que, qujnmama in jntevoan cemjlhujtl qujmjtztiuj, in ixqujchtin tiacahoan, in tequjoaque, no cemjlhujtl qujmjtztiuj, in jxqujch iauqujzquj in tenochcatl, no cemjlhujtl qujmjtztiuj, in jxqujch iauqujzquj tlati-lulcatl: no cemjlhujtl qujmjtztiuj, in jxqujch acul-hoacatl: no cemjlhujtl qujtztiuj, in jxqujch tepane-catl, no cemjlhujtl qujtztiuj, ixilotepecatl: no cemjl-hujtl q'mjtztiuj, in jxqujch moquataitoa: çan no iuj in oc cequj altepetl, motetecpana, iujian, iocuxca, in otlatoca.

Auh in jcoac, oaxioac teuatenpan, tlachinoltempan, in iehoantin tiacaoan tlatlacuchcalca, tlatlacatecca njman teumaca, tetecpana, aiac vel tepanauja, aiac vel tetlan qujça, çan njman vncã qujnmjctia, qujnuj-ujtequj, in aqujn tlaixneloznequj: tetlan qujçazne-quj, in oommoten ixqujch iauqujzquj, in ie inman in ooalhuetz acaujztli, in tlaioalli injc tlaiooalcujoaz: auh in jcoac ie itech nequetzaloz, in altepetl poliujz, achto oc cenca mochiia in tletl, in quenman cue-

2. The corresponding Spanish passage reads: "*Mandaua luego, a los calpisques, que lleuassen armas, a todos los principales, para si, y para sus soldados: y entonce lo notificaua a su gentes, y los dauan armas.*"

3. *Teuatenpan, tlachinoltempan:* cf. Sahagún, *op. cit.,* II, p. 103 *(lugares para la guerra señalados),* and p. 105 *(los lugares de las batallas).*

And when they already were to rise against the city to destroy it, first was awaited tensely the moment when fire flared up—when the priests brought forth [new] fire—and for the blowing of shell trumpets, when the priests blew them.

And when the fire flared up, then as one arose all the warriors. War cries were raised; there was fighting. They shot fiery arrows into the temples.

And when they first took a captive, one fated to die, forthwith they slew him there before the gods; they slashed his breast open with a flint knife.

And when the city had been overcome, thereupon were counted as many captives as there were, and as many Mexicans and Tlatilulcans as had died. Then they apprised the ruler that they had been orphaned for the sake of Uitzilopochtli; that men had been taken captive and been slain. And the ruler then commanded the high judges to go to tell and inform all in the homes of those who had gone to die in war, that there might be weeping in the homes of those who had gone to war to die. And they informed those in the homes of as many as had gone to take captives in war that they had received honors there because of their valor. And they were rewarded according to their merits; the ruler accorded favors to all—costly capes, breech clouts, chocolate, food, and devices, and labrets and ear plugs. Even more did the ruler accord favors to the princes if they had taken captives. He gave them the offices of stewards, and all wealth without price—honor, fame, renown.

And if some had done wrong in battle, they then and there slew them on the battlefield; they beat them, they stoned them.

And if several claimed one captive, and one man said, "He is my captive," and another man also said, "He is my captive": if no man verified it, and also if no one saw how they had taken the captive, the lord of the sun decided between them. If neither had an advantage of the two who claimed the captive, then those who had taken four captives, the masters of the captives, decided that to neither one would the captive belong. He was dedicated to the Uitzcalco[4] [or] they left him to the *calpulco,* the house of the devil.

And when the city which they had destroyed was attained, at once was set the tribute, the impost. [To the ruler who had conquered them] they gave that

ponjz: injc tlequauhtlaça tlamacazque: ioã in tlapitzalli in tecuciztli, in oqujpitzque tlamacazque:

ioan in ocuepon tletl, njman ic cemeoa, in jxqujch iauquizquj, motempapauja, mjcali, qujtlemjna in teucalli.

Auh in achto in caçi malli in maliacatl, çan njman vncan, imjxpan qujmjctia, in teteu, tecpatica queltetequj.

Auh in jcoac ompoliuh altepetl, njmã ie ic nemalpoalo, in quexqujch malli: ioan in quexqujch omjc mexicatl, in tlatilulcatl, njman muchi qujcaqujtia in tlatoanj, injc tepal oicnopiltic vitzilobuchtli injc otlamaloc, ioan omjcoac: auh in tlatoanj njman qujnnaoatia, in tecutlatoque: injc qujtemachtitiuj, injc qujtecaqujtitiuj, in jnchan in jzqujnti, oiaumjqujto, injc choqujlilozque in jnchachan, in oiaumjqujto: ioan qujtecaqujtia in jnchan, in quezquj otlamato iauc, ic vncan qujcujia in maujziotl, in jpampa oqujchiotl: ioan qujmomaceujaia in jxqujch iteicneliaia in tlatoanj, in tlaçotilmatli, in maxtlatl, in atl, tlaqualli, ioan tlaujztli, ioan teçacatl, nacochtli: oc cenca qujmjcneliaia in tlaçopipilti, in tlatoanj intla otlamato, qujmaca calpixcantli: ioan in jxqujch tlaçotli necujltonolli, in maujziotl, in tleiotl, in teiotl.

Auh intla acame qujtlacoa iauiotl, njman vmpa qujnmjctia in iauc qujnviujtequj, qujntetepachoa.

Auh intla acame, qujmocujcujlia ce malli, qujtoa ce tlacatl, ca nomal, in oc ce tlacatl no qujtoa ca nomal: intlacamo ce tlacatl itech nelti, aiac no qujmjttac, in quenjn tlamaque: iehoantin qujntlatzontequjlia, in tonatiuh itlatocahoan: aiac tle onqujça in jmomextin in qujmocujcujlia in malli: iuh qujtzontequj, in quauhtlatoque, in mallatoque, aiac ce itech pouhquj iez in malli: vitzcalli qujpoaia, calpolco qujcaoaia, in jchan tlacateculotl.

Auh in jcoac oaxioac altepetl in ovmpoliuh, njman icoac motlalia, in tequjtl, in tlacalaqujlli itech mana in tlein vmpa muchioa, auh njman no iquac ixque-

---

4. Cf. *ibid.,* pp. 381-382, referring to the *barrio* of Coatlan, where slaves fought and died in sacrifice: *"Esto era en el patio del templo que se dice Uitzcalco."*

which was there made. And likewise, forthwith a steward was placed in office, who would watch over and levy the tribute.

SECOND PARAGRAPH, in which it is described how they chose judges.

The ruler watched especially over the trials; he heard all the accusations and the complaints, the afflictions, and the misery of the common folk, the orphans, the poor, and the vassals.

And in order that the ruler might verify one's accusations and guilt, there were placed in office, and [the ruler] chose, as his judges,[5] the princes, those who were endowed with the necessities of life, those provided with drink and food—the rich; and the brave warriors and men [at arms], who had been reared in war and had gloried in all kinds of suffering and misery. In all things had their upbringing, their rearing, been sound. In their infancy they had been taught [according to] the upbringing in the priests' house, or the rearing by the masters of the youths, growing up with others, living in the [same] houses as others, engaging in war, taking captives.

And likewise the ruler thus chose and placed in office judges of the Mexicans who were not noblemen—those of sound and righteous upbringing, who had been reared in war: brave warriors and men [at arms] who in many ways had won glory by the favor of the ruler. By his grace they drank and ate. He gave them contentment and he gave them gifts; he bestowed upon them whatsoever they needed.

Such as these the ruler gave office and chose as his judges—the wise, the able, the sage; who listened and spoke well; who were of good memory; who spoke not vainly nor lightly; who did not make friends without forethought nor were drunkards; who guarded their lineage with honor; who slept not overmuch, [but rather] arose early; who did nothing for friendship's or kinship's sake, nor for enmity; who would not hear nor judge a case for a fee. The ruler might condemn them to death; hence they performed their offices as judges righteously. For otherwise, these judges could find excuse for the wrongs which they might do.

And when the ruler placed his judges in office, he gave them two court rooms, the Teccalli, where they

tzalo in calpixquj, in qujmocujtlaujz, in jpan tlatoz in tlacalaqujlli.

INJC VME PARRAPHO: ipan mjtoa, in quenjn qujnpepenaia Iuezes.

In tlatoanj oc cenca qujmocujtlaujaia in tetlatzontequjliliztli, qujcaquja in jxqujch in jneteilhujl: ioan in jchoqujz, in jnentlamachiliz in jnetolinjliz in cujtlapilli, atlapalli in jcnotlacatl, in motolinja in maçeoalli:

auh injc uel qujnneltiliaia in tlatoanj in teneteilhujl anoço tetlatlacul qujmjxquetzaia, qujnpepenaia in jtecutlatocahoan: iehoantin in tlaçopipilti, in tlaiecultilo in oncã in qujnj, in qujquanj, in mocujltonoa, ioan tiacaoan, oqujchti, in iauc omozcaltique, mjiec tlamãtli tecoco netolinjliztli, oqujmaujçoque: auh in jzquj tlamantlj qualli neoapaoaliztli, nezcaltiliztli, in jnpiltian oqujmomachtique, in calmecac neoapaoaliztli, in tiachcapa neoapaoaliztli, in tetlan neoapaoaliztli, in calpan tetlan nemjliztli, iauqujçaliztli, tlamaliztli.

Auh çan no iuhquj, injc qujnpepenaia tlatoanj, inic qujmjxquetzaia in tecutlatoque, in mexica, in amo pipilti iehoantin in qualli iectli, inneoapaoaliz, innezcaltiliz, in iauc omooapauhque, in tiacahoan in oqujchti, in mjiec tlamantli oqujmaujçoque, iteicneliliz tlatoanj, in jpal atli, tlaqua, in qujnpaqujltia, in qujntlauhtia, ioan in qujnmaca, in jxqujch intech monequj:

iuhque in in qujmjxquetzaia, in qujnpepenaia tlatoanj, in jtecutlatocahoan, in mjmatinj, in mozcalianj, in tlanemjlianj, in vellacaquj, in vellatoa, in motlaiollotianj, in amo ahaujllatoa, in amo cacamanaloa, in amo iliujz 'moocnjuhtia, amo tlaoananj, cenca qujmaujzpia in tecuiotl, amo cochinj, cenca cochiçanj amo tle qujcnjuhchioa: amo tle qujoaiolcachioa: amo tle qujtecocolicachioa, amo tlaxtlaujltica qujcaquj, anoço qujtzontequj: qujmjqujznaoatiaia, in tlatoanj: injc melaoac qujchioazque in jntequjuh, in tecutlatollj: auh intlacamo, ca iehoantin conmotzacujlitiazque in tecutlatoque, in tlein qujtlacozque.

Auh in jcoac, oqujmjxquetz in tlatoanj: in jtecutlatocahoan qujnmacaia vntetl in tlatocacalli, in tec-

---

5. *Jtecutlatocahoan:* cf. *ibid.,* p. 318 (*los mayores jueces*) and p. 321 (*senadores*).

were to remain, to make judgments, and to hear all manner of testimony.

The name of one Teccalli was Tlacxitlan. There they tried princes and great lords. At once, swiftly, they passed judgment on their complaints or wrong doing.

And the second place where justice was done was named Teccalli. There were the Mexican judges. Sagely they heard the complaints of the common folk. They defined and verified the complaint, they recorded it in paintings so that they might take it there to Tlacxitlan, where they informed the judges who were princes, so that there judgment might be pronounced.

And if something was difficult, they took it to the ruler so that he might judge it [with] those judges[6] whose names were Ciuacoatl, Tlacochcalcatl, Uitznauatlailotlac, Ticociauacatl, Pochtecatlailotlac, Ezuauacatl,[7] Mexicatl tezcacoacatl, Acatliacapanecatl, Milnauatl, Atlauhcatl, Ticociauacatl, Ciuatecpanecatl, and Tequixquinaoacatl. These same judges meditated and pondered upon, and examined, the testimony. They sought out the witnesses, those who bore testimony. Perchance [the charge] was true; or else that which the ruler had heard was false, so that, perhaps, by error[8] someone had been held in jail.

And if the ruler condemned someone to die, then his executioners slew him—the Achcacauhti,[9] the Quauhnochtli, and the Atempanecatl. Thus did these slay him: with a cord they strangled the evildoer, or they stoned him before the people, or they cut him to pieces.

THIRD PARAGRAPH, in which is described how all were to dance.

The ruler was greatly concerned with the dance, the rejoicing, in order to hearten and console all the peers, the noblemen, the lords, the brave warriors, and all the common folk and vassals.

First the ruler announced what song should be intoned. He commanded the singers to rehearse and practise the song and [to prepare] the two-toned

calli, in vncan iezque, in vncã tetlatzontequjlizque, in vncan qujcaqujzque in jxqujch tlamãtli tlacatlatolli,

in centetl teccalli, itoca tlacxitlan, in vncã tetlatzontequjliaia tlaçopipilti, tlatocapipilti, çan njman içiuhca qujtzontequja inteneteilhujl, anoço tetlatlacul.

Auh injc vccan tecutlatoloia, itoca teccalli, vncan catca in tecutlatoque mexica: iujian iocuxca qujcaqujia, in jneteilhujl cujtlapilli, atlapalli, in oqujchipauhque, in oqujiectilique neteilhujlli, tlapallacujlolpan qujtlalia, injc vmpa qujtquj tlacxitlan in jpã qujntlapoujlia in tecutlatoque in tlaçopipilti, injc vmpa motzontequj.

Auh intla itla oujlitica iujc qujtquj in tlatoanj injc iehoanti qujtzontequj in jntoca catca tecutlatoque. Çioacoatl tlacochcalcatl, vitznaoatlailotlac, ticociaoacatl, pochteca tlailotlac, ezoaoacatl, mexicatl tezcacoacatl, acatliacapanecatl, mjlnaoatl, atlauhcatl, ticociaoacatl, çioatecpanecatl, tequjxqujnaoacatl, iehoantin, y, in tecutlatoque qujnemjliaia, qujchiquja, qujpetlaoaia in tlacatlatolli, qujntemoaia in machiceque, in tlaneltilianj, in aço ie nelli, anoço tlatolchichioalli in caqujtilo tlatoanj, in aço can tlapic aca quauhcalco otlaliloc.

Auh intla aca qujtlatzontequjlia tlatoanj mjqujz, njman qujmjctia, in jtemjcticaoan achcacauhti, quauhnochtli, atempanecatl: injc iehoantin qujmjctia, qujmecanja in tlatlacoanj, anoço teixpan qujtetepachoa, anoço qujtetequj.

INJC EI PARRAPHO: ipan mjtoa in quenjn netotiloz.

In tlatoanj oc cenca qujmocujtlaujaia, in maçeoaliztli, in papaqujliztli, injc qujmellaquaoa, injc qujniollalia, in jxqujchtin tlatoque, ioan pipilti, ioan tetecuti, ioan tiacahoan: ioan in jxqujch in cujtlapilli, atlapalli, in maçeoalli:

achtopa qujtoaia in tlatoanj, in tlein cujcatl meoaz, qujnnaoatiaia in cujcanjme: injc qujiehecozque injc qujchicaoazque in cujcatl, ioan teponaztli, olmaitl,

6. The corresponding Spanish text reads: "Y los casos, muy dificultosos, y graues, lleuauanlos al señor: para que los sentenciasse juntamente con treze principales, muy calificados, que con el andauan, y residian."

7. After the word pochtecatlailotlac, the Real Academia de la Historia MS includes mixcoatlatlalotlac; ezoaoacatl appears as eçiuauacatl. The title Ticociauacatl is repeated in the Aztec text of the Florentine Codex.

8. Can tlapic: çan is probably meant (cf. ibid.).

9. Achcacauhti: cf. Sahagún, op. cit., I, pp. 166, 291, 293; II, pp. 310, 321; also Anderson and Dibble, op. cit., II, p. 100, and III, p. 53.

drums, the rubber drum hammers, and the ground drums, and all the properties used in the dance. And [he appointed the kind of] dance, him who would give the pitch, those who would lead, him who would beat the two-toned drum, him who would play the ground drum. All was first arranged, so that nothing would be left out.

And when there was a dance, the ruler [decided] the day. At this time, he adorned and arrayed himself, [in his] head band with sprays of quetzal feathers and gold, with which he bound his hair; a yellow labret, or a green stone lip plug, which he inserted in his [lower] lip; golden ear plugs, which he inserted in [the lobes of] his ears; and he laid on a neck band, either a neck band of green stone or a collar with turquoise inserted; he placed on his wrist a bracelet with a large green stone upon it, or a large turquoise; or a golden arm band; and a quetzal feather fan. With [these] costly goods he went in procession and danced. With a priceless cape he covered and wrapped himself, and in a costly breech clout he girt himself.

Then also they arrayed and accorded favors to all the lords, and noblemen, the men [at arms], brave warriors, and the high judges, and the [lesser] judges, and brave warriors, men [at arms], and masters of the youths, and singers. And the ruler gave them drink and food, all the things which have been mentioned.

And if the singers did something amiss—perchance a two-toned drum was out of tune, or a ground drum; or he who intoned, marred the song; or the leader marred the dance—then the ruler commanded that they place in jail whoever had done the wrong; they imprisoned him, and he died.

FOURTH PARAGRAPH, in which is told how he who was the ruler kept vigil; how he kept guard at night and all day, because of war.

The ruler was especially concerned with the keeping of watch against enemies and the guarding of the city, all day and all night. Hence he gave stern commands that guard should be kept faithfully. For at times, suddenly, the City of Mexico was circled by *foes*; perchance somewhere for this they were gathered together, and were laying a snare. Therefore the ruler kept careful vigil. He did not become besotted. He himself sometimes set forth by night, circled the city, and beheld what was done: perhaps the priest

veuetl: ioan in ixqujch maçeoallatqujtl, ioan netotiliztli, aqujn cujcaitoz, aqujque in teiacanazque, aqujn teponaçoz, aqujn veuetzonaz, mochi achto mocencaoaia injc atle itlacaujz.

Auh in ie icoac maçeoa tlatoanj, in tlein ilhujtl ipan mocencaoa, mochichioa quetzallalpilonj coztic teucujtlaio, injc qujlpia itzon, coztic teçacatl, anoço chalchiuhtentetl in conaquja itenco, coztic teucujtlanacochtli, in caquja inacazco: auh in cozcatl conteca, aço chalchiuhcozcatl, anoço cozcapetlatl, teuxiujtl itlaactoc, macuextli imac qujtlalia vei chalchiujtl ipan ca anoço vej teuxiujtl, anoço coztic teucujtlamatemecatl, quetzalecaceoaztli, tlaçotlanquj injc mjtotia injc maceoa, tlaçotilmatli in qujmololoa, in qujmoquentia, tlaçomaxtlatl in qujmomaxtlatia,

njman ic no qujcencaoa qujntlauhtia: in ixqujchtin tlatoque, ioan pipilti, in oqujchti, tiiacaoan, ioan tecutlatoque, ioan achcacauhti, ioan tiiacaoan oqujchtin, ioan tiachcaoan, ioan cujcanjme, ioan qujnmaca in jiauh, in jtlaqual tlatoanj in jzqujtlamantin omoteneuhque.

Auh intla itla qujtlacoa cujcanjme: aço teponaztli qujchalanja, anoço veuetl, anoço cujcaitoa, qujpoloa cujcatl: anoço teiacana, in qujpoloa netotiliztli: njman tlanaoatia in tlatoanj, quauhcalco contlalia in aqujn tlatlacoa, qujtzacutiuh mjquja.

INJC NAUJ PARRAPHO: vncã mjtoa injc ixtoçoaia in aqujn tlatoanj, injc tlapiaia in ioaltica: ioan in cemjlhujtl in jpãpa iauiotl.

In tlatoanj oc cenca qujmocujtlaujaia in iautlapializtli, ioan altepepializtli, cemjlhujtl ceioal, ic tlatlaquauhnaoatiaia, injc cenca tlapialoz ma quenmanjan atenemachpan iauiaoalolo in altepetl mexico, aço cana ica necentlalilo, tlachichiujlilo, ipampa cenca ixtoçoaia in tlatoanj, amo tlaoanaia, iioma in iohoaltica quenmanjan qujçaia qujiaoaloa in altepetl qujtta tlein muchioa, acaçomo tlapia in tlamacazquj in tiachcauh aço ie necujtlaujlo in mjxitl in tlapatl in octli ioan oc cenca qujntlaquauhnaoatiaia in tlatoanj

or the master of the youths were not keeping watch, having already become addlepated.[10] And the ruler most sternly commanded that all the seasoned warriors and lords keep watch all day and all night in warlike lands and be concerned to be a rampart of men dexterous at arms in enemy paths. And they were to apprehend and seize informers who had entered here in secret, who walked about the city. And they perceived when war was to be proclaimed. And when war already was declared, then they hastened to enter [their city] to warn their lords so that then they would ready themselves for guarding against the foe.

And if informers[11] were seized, they were slain; they were beaten, because of what they made known. And if it were noted that some knew the Mexicans and were living with them in their homes, they also imprisoned the informers of the ruler's foes, with the householders who had been plotting with them, and their children, and plundered their goods, so that nothing[12] was to be seen in their homes.

And likewise the ruler urged strongly that watch be kept within the city, all day and all night, lest someone betray the city, lest it might be surrounded by enemies. And therefore sometimes the ruler and the city would march forth. And the ruler commanded that rulers of the youths, the brave warriors, and all the youths, each day, at night, should sing and dance, so that all the cities which lay around Mexico should hear. For the ruler slept not, nor any of the Mexicans.

And when it was deep night, then the priests of Tenochtitlan and of Tlatilulco, and [men from] all the hamlets [nearby], blew shell trumpets and beat two-toned drums. Then all the priests went forth. Everywhere they performed penances all about the mountain tops. And thus they kept watch lest they come upon something. [When] already it grew light, they went into [the city]. Thus they kept guard each night; thus did they do.

in jxqujchtin iauteoaque in tlatoque icemjlhujtl içeiooal tlapiazque, in teuatenpan in tlachinoltempã, in qujmocujtlaujzque oçelotenamjtl, quauhtenamjtl, in iauotli: ioan qujmanazque qujntzitzqujzque in tetlan nenque in ichtaca oalcalaquj in qujoalnemilia altepetl, ioan oallapia in jqujn iautlatoloz, auh in oqujcacque ca ie iautlatolo: njman calactiuetzi in connonotza intlátocauh inic njman no moçencaoa iautlapializtica.

Auh intla ano tetlanenque, mjctilo, tetzotzonalo inca nenonotzalo. Auh intla macho, ca acame qujmati in mexica in inchan oalmocallotia, in tetlanenque in jiaohoan no qujtzacutiuja, inca nenonotzaloia in chaneque, ioã in jnpilhoan, ioan namoieloia in intlatquj atl neneçia in inchan.

Auh çan no iuhquj cenca ipan tlatoaia in tlatoanj injc cenca tlapializoz in jitic altepetl, icemjlhujtl, çeioal, in ma aca qujtlachichiujli altepetl, in ma iauiaoalolo quenmanjan, auh injc icatiaz tlatoanj, ioan altepetl qujnnaoatiaia in tlatoanj in telpuchtlatoque, in tiacahoan: ioan in ixqujch telpuchtli, injc momoztlae ioaltica cujcoanozque, injc qujoalcaqujz ixqujch altepetl, in qujiaoalotoc mexico: ca amo cochi in tlatoanj, ioan ixqujch mexicatl.

Auh in jquac tlaquauhtlapoiaoa: njman tlapitza, ioan teponaçohoa, in tlamacazque tenochca, ioan tlatilulca: ioan ixqujch altepemaitl, icoac qujça in jxqujchtin tlamacazque, noujian in ontlamaçeoa noujian tepeticpac, ioan ic ontlapia in aço itla qujnamjqujtiuj ie tlatujnaoac ỹ oalcalaquja injc ontlapiaia çeçeioal iuh qujchioaia.

---

10. Siméon, op. cit., identifies mixitl as an intoxicating plant, and tlapatl as Ricinnus communis, a medicinal plant. Olmos, op. cit., p. 223, has, for Hazer a otro vellaco, o dar mal consejo: Mixitl, tlapatl, coaxuxuhqui, nanacatl nicteittinemi. . . .; for Emborrachose, o salio de seso: Ytech oquiz in uctli, in nanacatl, in mixtli, in coaxuxuhqui inic oyuintic, inic oxocomic. In Lib. VI, fol. 209r, of the Florentine Codex, this passage appears: "In ticicatinemj, in timeltzotzontinemj: in juhquj mjxitl, in juhquj tlapatl otiqujc. Itechpa mjtoaia: in aqujn aiocmo qujcaqujznequj tenenetzaliztli: ca iuhquj in ma tlaoanquj, ma tlapatl oqujqua: injc nemj: aiocmo qujlnamjquj in tlein ic nonotzaloia: ipampa injc aioia, in amo muzcalia: ilviloia. Tlein mach oticqua, tlein mach oticpapalo: aioc vel mjtzcaoa, aiocmo qujtlalcavia in moiollo: in aiocmo ticcuj, ticana in tlatolli." The corresponding Spanish text reads: "Esta letra qujere dezir. Andas azezando y dandote palmadas en el pecho como hombre que a comjdo belleños. Por metaphora se dize: de aquel que siendo traujeso y desbaratado en su viujr, siendo coregido, no se qujere emendar: y a este tal dizenle que as beujdo que as comjdo que njngun bien cosejo rescibe tu coraçon."

11. Tetlan nenque: sentinels, according to Siméon, op. cit. Tetlannemini, however, in Molina, op. cit., is translated as chismero or malsin (gossip, talebearer; hence, possibly, informer).

12. Atl: probably atle is meant.

And in the great palace, the ruler's residence, likewise was watch kept all night. Never did the fire go out. It was watched all night and made to burn with pine torches there in the residence of the ruler—at the Tlacxitlan, and the Teccalli, and the Tecpilcalli, the Quauhcalli, the Achcauhcalli, the Cuicacalli, the Coacalli, and the residences of the lords throughout the city, and the priests' houses, and the majordomos' houses—where assembled the majordomos,—and the young men's houses which were placed in all the neighborhoods.[13] Then the youths filled the houses as they kept guard. None slept in his [own] home. The task of the youths was to go into the forest, in order that watch be kept within the city; for nightly there was light and fires were burned; thus was guard maintained.

FIFTH PARAGRAPH, in which is told how the ruler was amused.

The ruler, when he beheld and knew that the common folk and vassals were very fretful, then commanded that the ball game be played, in order to animate the people and divert them. He commanded the majordomos to take out the rubber ball, and the girdles, and the leather hip guards, and the leather gloves with which the ruler's ball players were dressed and arrayed. And things were arranged on the ball court; there was sprinkling, there was sanding, there was sweeping.

And all which the ruler was to wager in the game —the valued capes, the duck feather capes, the costly breech clouts, the green stone lip plugs, the golden ear plugs, the green stone necklaces, the golden necklaces, the wrist bands with large, precious,[14] green stones upon them, and all the precious capes and bedding—the majordomos brought out and placed in the ball court. And those who were to challenge and play ball against the ruler then matched all his costly goods. And all the poor folk placed [for] the ruler, each one, old capes like those which the vassals wore. And if they won from the ruler, then the majordomos brought out others and laid out all the costly goods which they had won of the ruler, and also they gave to the vassals all which they had won of the ruler.

Auh in vei tecpan in tlatoca, çan no iuhquj ceioal in tlapialoia, aquenman ceuja in tletl: çeioal in tlapialoia, ioan tlaujloia ocotica, in vncan iieian tlatoanj, ioan tlacxitlan, ioan teccali, ioã tecpilcalli, quauhcali, achcauhcali, cujcacali, ioan coacali, in jntenetlaliaian tlatoque altepetl ipan, ioan calmecac, ioan texãcali in jnneçenqujxtiaia calpixque, ioan telpuchcali, in noujian tlâtlâxilacalpan mamanj: vncã icacaltemj in telpupuchti in tlapia, aiac ichan oncochia, intequjuh catca in telpopochti, in quauhtla ializtli, injc tlapieloia iitic altepetl injc çeçeioal tlaujloia tlatlatiloia, injc tlapieloia.

INJC MACUJLLI PARRAPHO: ipan mitoa, in quenjn mellelqujxtiaia, tlatoanj.

In tlatoanj in jcoac qujttaia, qujmatia ca cenca nentlamati in cujtlapilli, atlapalli maceoalli: njman tlanaoatiaia, injc ollamaloz, injc teellaquaoaia, injc tepaqujltiaia tlatoanj: qujnnaoatiaia in calpixque, injc qujoalcujzque in olli, ioan nelpilonj, ioan queçeoatl, ioan maieoatl: injc mocencaoa injc mochichioa, in jollancaoan tlatoanj, ioan tlacencaoalo in tlachco, tlaaujlilo, tlaxalujlo, tlachpano:

ioan in jxqujch qujtlanjtoz tlatoanj, in tlaçotilmatli in xomoiujtilmatli, in tlaçomaxtlatl, in chalchiuhtentetl, teucujtlanacochtli, chalchiuhcozcatl, teucujtlacozcatl, matzopetztli chalchiujtl vei ipan ca, tlaçotl: ioan in ixqujch tlaçotilmatli, ioan pepechtli qujoalqujxtia in calpixque, qujoallalia in tlachco. Auh in iehoantin qujnamjqujzque, in collamjzque tlatoanj: njman jq'tiamjctia, in jxqujch itlatquj tlaçotli: auh in ie ix motolinja maceoalli, iceceiaca contlalia tlatoanj ica iiaiaçol in iuhquj qujqquemj maçeoalli. Auh intla oqujtlanque tlatoanj, njman tepatla, in calpixque qujtema in ixqujch tlaçotli tlatqujtl, in oqujtlanjlique tlatoanj: auh in maceoalti no qujnmaca in jxqujch oqujtlanilique tlatoanj.

13. *Tlatlaxilacalpan:* see Arturo Monzón: *El calpulli en la organización social de los tenochca* (México: Instituto de Historia, 1949), p. 51, where the term *tlaxilacalli* is defined as a small *barrio* or street. According to Orozco y Berra, *op. cit.,* I, p. 369, *"los pueblos quedaron subdivididos en tantos* calpulli *ó barrios, cuantas las parcialidades eran, cada* calpulli *dividido por calles ó* tlaxilacalli."

14. *Tlaçotl:* the corresponding Spanish text refers to slaves, in which case the Aztec should read *tlacotl.*

When he wished to be amused, the ruler commanded that they play *patolli,* that a mat on which *patolli* was played be painted black, in widely spaced stripes. So was it painted that there might be kept the count whereby the game could be won. And then also holes were drilled into the surfaces of four large beans with which *patolli* was played and the game was won. And in the same way the majordomos did [as in the ball game]:[15] they spread out all the costly goods and belongings of the ruler, there where *patolli* was played, where [players] represented the ruler. And then, if the ruler were bested, then the majordomos brought out other [players]; and they changed all the vassals whom the ruler had set in place that *patolli* be played.

SIXTH PARAGRAPH, in which is described the ruler who was good of heart and kindly.

The ruler was very indulgent of others, very merciful, and kindly. When he wished, he set forth along the road, following it. If any poor vassal, who made bold to hail the ruler, greeted him pleasingly, then [the ruler] commanded the majordomo to give him a cape, a breech clout, and a place for him to sleep, and that which he might drink, and eat—dried grains of maize, beans, amaranth seed. And if a lowly woman made bold to greet the ruler, he likewise granted and accorded her her shift, her skirt, a place for her to sleep, what she might drink and eat—grains of dried maize, beans, amaranth seed. And if some poor indigent were to fashion or make so many skin drums, or a song of honor, if then he dedicated them to the ruler, if he gave them [to him, the ruler] showed great compassion and indulged him; he gave him a house, he enriched him; he gave him whatsoever goods lay in the house; and he gave him a steward who daily might care for him, give him to eat, provide him his breakfast, wherewith to break his fast, and provide him wherewith to sup. And he gave him all [manner of] gifts—costly capes, beds, wealth, women, and a slave, and honor.

In tlatoanj, in jquac qujnequja iiellelqujçaz tlanaoatiaia injc patoz, mjcujloa ce patolpetlatl, ica tlilli, papatlactic in tlaxotlalli ic mjcujloa, in vncan nepoalo ic netlanjoa: auh njman no mjxcoionja nauhtetl aiecotli, injc patolo injc netlanjoa: auh çan ie no iuhquj qujchioaia in calpixque, injc mochi tlaçotli in jtlatquj, in jaxca tlatoanj, qujoalteca in oncan patoloian, in qujtetlanitalhuja in tlatoanj, auh in icoac, intla otlanjhoac tlatoanj, njman tepatla in calpixque: ioan qujp̄patla in jxqujchtin maçeoalti, in ocontlalica tlatoanj in patoloia.

INJC CHIQUACEN PARRAPHO: vncan mjtoa, in aqujn tlatoanj qualli iiollo, teicnoittanj.

In tlatoanj, cenca tetlaoculianj, cenca teicnoittanj, ioan teicnelianj, in jcoac qujnequja, qujçaz in otli qujtocaz: in aqujn motolinja maçeoalli, in motlapaloa, injc qujtlapaloz tlatoanj, intla ouelqujtlapalo in tlatoanj: njman qujnaoatia in calpixquj, qujmacaz tilmatli, maxtlatl, ioan icochia, ioan in qujz, in qujquaz, tlaolli, etl, oauhtli. Auh intla motolinjanj çioatl motlapaloz qujtlapaloz tlatoanj, çan no iuh qujcnelia, qujtlauhtia in jujpil, in jcue, icochia, in qujz, in qujquaz tlaolli, etl, oauhtli. Auh intla aca motolinja, icnotlacatl, oqujchiuh, oqujtlali, quezquj veuetl maujzio cuicatl, intla njman itech qujpoa tlatoanj, intla qujmaca, cenca qujcnelia, qujtlaocolia, qujcalmaca qujcujltonoa, qujmaca in quexqujch tlatqujtl in jitic onoc calli, ioan qujmaca calpixquj injc momoztlae qujmocujtlaujz qujtlaqualtiz, qujtenjxitiz, qujneuhcaiotiz qujcochcaiotiz: ioan qujmaca in ixqujch netlauhtilli in tlaçotilmatli, in pepechtli in necujltonolli, çioa, ioan tlacotli, ioan mauiziotl.

15. Cf. corresponding Spanish text: *"y de alli tenjan su iuego, con que perdian, y ganauan ioyas: y otras cosas como arriba se dixo."*

Eighteenth Chapter, in which it is told how they chose those who would govern.

The ruler was thus given office and chosen. The lords assembled and deliberated as to whom they would set in office and choose to be ruler. In the same manner assembled the old men and the seasoned warriors, brave warriors, men [at arms], and the leaders of the youths; lords; and keepers of the gods; fire priests—the long-haired ones.[1] All were gathered there at the great palace, the residence of the ruler, in order to consult and choose him who was to be ruler. They cast votes for all the princes who were sons of lords; men [at arms]; brave warriors, experienced in war, who shrank not from the enemy;[2] who knew not wine—who were not drunkards, who became not stupefied;[3] the prudent, able, wise; of sound and righteous rearing and upbringing; who spoke well and were obedient, benevolent, discreet, and intelligent.

And when were settled the deliberations and choosing, they were as one [in their] accord. When a certain prince was chosen and given the charge of being ruler, then also were raised to their office and chosen those who were to help him, the [four] princes who would be by his side; who would be his lords. They were invested with, and given, the titles Tlacochcalcatl, Uitznauatlailotlac, Pochtecatla-ilotlac, and Ticociauacatl.

When this was done, when the choosing was settled, then was determined on what good day sign would be installed those who had been elected—the ruler and the lords. Then the command was given when there would be a meeting, and all the noblemen were commanded then to come to assemble in the courtyard of the Temple of Uitzilopochtli.

Injc caxtolli omej capitulo: ipan mjtoa, in quenjn qujnpepenaia, in aqujque tlatocatizque.

In tlatoanj, injc ixquetzaloia, inic pepenaloia, mocentlaliaia, mononotzaia, in tecutlatoque, injc qujxquetzaia, injc qujpepenaia, in aqujn tlatoanj iez çan no iuhquj mocentlaliaia in achcacauhti ioan tequjoaque, tiacahoan, oqujchtin, ioan tiachcauh tlatoque, ioã teupixque tlenamacaque, papaoaque, ixqujchtin mocentlaliaia in vncan vei tecpan tlatocan, injc mononotzaia, injc qujpepenaia in ac iehoatl tlatocatiz, qujnteneoaia in jxqujchtin tlaçopipilti, in tlatoque impilhoan, in oqujchtin, in tiacaoan in iauc matinj, in amo qujtlaçotla in jntzontecõ, in jmelchiqujuh, in amo qujximati in vctli, in amo tlaoananj, in amo qujmotequjtia mjxitl, tlapatl, in mjmatinj, in mozcalianj, in tlamatinj, in qualli iectli inezcaliliz, inneoapaoaliz, in vellatoa, in vellacaquj, in tetlaçotlanj, in jxe in iollo.

Auh in jcoac in omocencauh nenonotzaliztli, tlapepenaliztli, in ocentet tlatolli, in ac iehoatl tlaçopilli in oanoc, in oixquetzaloc in tlatoanj iez: njman no iquac ixquetzalo, pepenalo in qujpaleujzque, in jtlan iezque in tlaçopipilti, in jtecutlatocahoan iezque: motecutlalia, motocamaca tlacochcalcatl, vitznaoatla-ilotlac pochtecatlailotlac, ticociaoacatl:

in ie iuhquj in omocencauh tlapepenaliztli, njman nenonotzalo, tlein qualli cemjlhujtonalli in jpan tlalilozque, in opepenaloque: in tlatoanj ioan in tecutlatoque, ic tenaoatilo in jqujn cenqujxooaz: ioan naoatilo in jxqujchtin pipilti, injc cenqujçaqujuj in jitoalco vitzilopuchtli:

---

1. Cf. corresponding Spanish text: *"juntauanse los senadores que llamauan Tecutlatoque: y tambien los viejos del pueblo, que llamauan achcacauhti: y tambien los capitanes soldados viejos de la guerra, que llamauan iautequjoaque: y otros capitanes que eran principales, en las cosas de la guerra: y tambien los satrapas, que llamauan Tlenamacaque, o papaoaque."*

Papauaque: cf. Anderson and Dibble, *op. cit.,* III, Appendix, cap. ii. In Bernardino de Sahagún: *Histoire générale des choses de la Nouvelle-Espagne* (D. Jourdanet and Rémi Siméon, trs.; Paris: G. Masson, 1880), p. 533, n. 2, the term is thus explained: *" 'Ceux qui ont les cheveux tombant en touffe sur les oreilles'; singulier papaua, formé du substantif papatli, chevelure longue et en désordre."*

2. Cf. Anderson and Dibble, *op. cit.,* II, p. 114.

3. *Mjxitl, tlapatl:* see Chap. 17, n. 10, *supra.*

And some of the noblemen who feared the office of ruler hid themselves and took refuge [from those who might choose them].[4]

FIRST PARAGRAPH, in which is told how they arrayed those who had been elected when they did penance, and led them to the house of Uitzilopochtli.

And at this time were brought together, according to command, the noblemen, the lords, the masters of the youths [who were] leaders, and great judges. When these lords were assembled, then they commanded the keepers of the gods, the long-haired ones, to seek out and go to take among themselves, those who had been chosen: the one whom they had named ruler and those whom they had named lords. When they had been put in office, then the keepers of the gods, the long-haired ones, went to take, wheresoever he was, the one who had been vested in the office of ruler. Then they speedily laid hold of him; before them, all the people beheld him.

Then they took him before the lords. He went bare. They put on him a green,[5] sleeveless jacket. And they had him carry upon his back his tobacco gourd with green tassels. Then they veiled his face, they covered his head [with a] green fasting cape designed with bones. Then they gave him his green[5] cotton bag filled with incense and decorated with bones, and they put on him his new foam sandals with green toes. They placed in his hand his incense ladle, also painted with the skulls of the dead, and with paper pendants [on the handle].

And these long-haired ones, keepers of the gods, went to take the ruler, making him go up before [the image of] Uitzilopochtli. When they had brought the ruler to the top [of the pyramid temple], then he took incense, poured it into the incense ladle, in which there were live coals. Then he raised it before [the image of] Uitzilopochtli in order to perfume it. He stood always with his face covered by the fasting cape designed with bones. And all the common folk stood looking up at him. Trumpets were sounded; the shell trumpets were blown.

And these lords—the Tlacochcalcatl, the Uitznaua-tlailotlac, the Pochtecatlailotlac and the Ticociauacatl —the keepers of the gods, the long-haired ones, then also speedily adorned. Each one they dressed in his

auh in cequjntin in pipilti in qujmacaçi tlatocaiotl motlatia mjnaia.

INJC CE PARRAPHO: ipan mjtoa, in quenjn qujnchichioaia, in opepenaloque, in jpan tlamaçeoaia: ioan qujnujcaia, in jchan vitzilopuchtli.

Auh in ie iuhquj: in ocenqujxoac, in jcoac naoatilli, in pipilti, in tecutlatoque, in tiiachcauh tlaiacatique, ioan achcacauhti, in onecentecoc, in iehoanti tecutlatoque niman qujnnaoatia in teupixque, papaoaque, injc qujxtemozque injc tetzalan conanatiuj: in opepenaloc in tlatoanj, qujtocaiotia in aqujn, ioan qujntocaiotia in aqujque tecutlatoque, oixquetzaloque njman ic uj in canazque in teupixque papaoaque, in campa catquj, oixquetzaloc tlatoanj: njman qujcujtiuetzi teixpan mochi tlacatl qujtta:

njman ie qujujca imjxpan tecutlatoque petlauhtiuh conaquja xicolli xoxouhquj, ioã qujmamaltia iietecon in jmamaxoxouhquj: njman ic conjxtlapachoa, ic qujquaqujmjloa neçaoalquachtli xoxoctic omjcallo, njmã ic conmana icpaxiqujpilli in vncan tentiuh copalli omjcallo xoxoctic: ioan conaaqujlia iancujc in jpoçolcac xoxoctic in jquequetzil, njman imac contequjlia, in jtlema, no mjccatzontecomaio, injc tlacujlolli, amocujtlapile.

Auh in iehoantin, papaoaque teupixque: caantiuj in tlatoanj in qujtlecauja ixpan vitzilopuchtli: in jcoac ocaxitique in tlatoanj, in tlacpac, njman concuj in copalli, contema in tlemaco, in vncan ietiuh tlexochtli: njman ic cacocuj in jxpan vitzilopuchtli, inic tlapopochuja, çan ic quatlapachiuhticac: in neçaoalquachtli, omjcallo. Auh in jxqujch maçeoalli, acopa conjtztoc, tlapitzalo, mopitza in tecuciztli.

Auh in iehoantin tecutlatoque, tlacochcalcatl, vitznaoatlailotlac, pochtecatlailotlac, ticociaoacatl: njman no hiçiuhca qujnchichioa, in teupixque papaoaque, ceceiaca qujmaquja tliltic ixicolli, ioan imjietecon,

4. Corresponding Spanish text: *"muchos de los que tenjan sospecha que los eligieran, se ascondiã por no ser electos por no tomar tan gran carga."*

5. *Xoxouhqui, xoxoctic: verde oscuro* in corresponding Spanish text.

black sleeveless jacket, and his tobacco gourd with black tassels, and they put on them their white foam sandals.[6] Then they veiled and covered their faces, each one of them, with black fasting capes designed with bones. And they gave them cotton incense bags, black and designed with bones, which they filled with incense. And their incense ladles were filled with live coals. Then also they took up each one of them; the keepers of the gods, the long-haired ones, went taking them in their midst, in order to have them go up above to [the Temple of] Uitzilopochtli. Then each one took incense; each one filled his incense ladle, which went full of live coals, and raised the incense ladle before [the image of] Uitzilopochtli and perfumed it.

SECOND PARAGRAPH, in which it is told how those chosen did penance there in the temple and came not forth for four days.

And when this was done, and they had offered incense and spread a fragrance before Uitzilopochtli, then they brought down the ruler, the lord of men; he went covered with the green fasting cape with a design of bones. Then they also brought down each one of the lords. They went quite slowly in order; they went with faces veiled, each one, with the fasting cape with the bone design.

The keepers of the gods, the long-haired ones, went taking them in their midst. They took [the ruler and] they escorted[7] [the lords] there to the house of fasting, a place named Tlacochcalco, or Tlacatecco, the house of Uitzilopochtli. There they fasted and did penance for four days. Nowhere went they forth; they only remained seated. When it was already midday, then the keepers of the gods, the long-haired ones, also went; the ruler and the lords in the Tlacatecco, who fasted there, they seized— they went taking them in their midst. They went with faces veiled in fasting capes; in the hands of each one went his incense ladle, and each one went taking with him his cotton bag filled with incense. Slowly and in order they went to take them up, above to [the Temple of] Uitzilopochtli, to offer incense, to spread a fragrance before [the image of] Uitzilopochtli. In the same way they came down; they came in order; they came with faces veiled in fasting capes designed with bones. Then was the time

tliltic in jmama, ioan qujmaaqujlia impocolcac iztac: njman ic qujmontlapachoa, qujmonixqujmjloa, cecenme, ica neçaoalquachtli, tliltic omjcallo, ioan qujmonmaca icpaxiqujpilli, tliltic omjcallo, in vncan temj copalli, ioan intlema tlexochtli ontentiuh: njman ic no qujntlecauja cecenme, qujntlacoaantiuj in teupixque papaoaque, injc qujntlecauja iicpac vitzilopuchtli, injc cecenme concuj in copalli, contema in jntlemaco, in vncan tentiuh tlexochtli, cacocuj in tlemaitl in jixpã vitzilopuchtli qujpopochuja.

INJC VME PARRAPHO: vncan mjtoa, in quenjn tlamaçeoaia in tlapepenalti, in vmpa teupan: auh amo oalqujçaia naujlhujtl.

Auh in ie iuhquj otlenamacaque, otlapopochujque iixpan vitzilopuchtli: njman ic qujoaltemouja in tlatoanj, tlacatecutli, tlapachiuhtiuh in jca neçaoalquachtli omjcallo xoxoctic: njman ic no ceceiaca qujnoaltemouja, in tecutlatoque, çan jujian tecpantiuj, ic ixtlapachiuhtiuj, ceceiaca in jca neçaoalquachtli omjcallo.

qujntlacoaantiuj in teupixque papaoaque, qujujca qujmonujca in neçaoalcalli, itocaiocan tlacochcalco, ioan tlacatecco, in jchan vitzilopuchtli: in vncan tlamaçeoaia moçaoaia naujlhujtl, amo campa qujça, çan eheoaticate; in jcoac ie nepantla tonatiuh, njman ic no ohuj in teupixque papaoaque: in vncan tlacatecco, in vncã moçaoaia tlatoanj, ioan tecutlatoque, qujmonana, qujntlacoaantiuj ixqujmjliuhtiuj, in jca neçaoalquachtli, inmac onotiuh in jntlema icecemme, ioan itlan cantiuh ceceiaca in jicpaxiqujpil, in vncan tentiuh copalli, çan jujian tecpantiuj, in qujntlecauja in jcpac vitzilopuchtli, inic ontlenamaca, injc ontlapopochhuja ixpan vitzilopuchtli: çan no iuj injc oaltemo tecpantiujtze, ixtlapachiuhtiujtze, in jca neçaoalquachtli omjcallo: qujnjcoac tlaqua in tlatoanj, ioã tecutlatoque ça ceppa in tlaqua cemjlhujtl.

---

6. *Impocolcac: impoçolcac* is meant.
7. The *Real Academia de la Historia MS* has *quimoncaua* for *qujmonujca*.

that the ruler and the lords ate; only once a day did they eat.

And at night, when midnight arrived, the ruler and the lords arose, covered with the fasting capes. And they took up their incense ladles and cotton bags filled with incense, and maguey spines; and they were shod in their foam sandals. And these keepers of the gods, the long-haired ones, took them in their midst—they took them above, to [the Temple of] Uitzilopochtli, to offer blood at midnight. And they offered incense; there they cast incense before [the image of] Uitzilopochtli.

In the same manner they came down. They went in order. The keepers of the gods, the long-haired ones, took them in their midst, with their faces veiled in fasting capes designed with bones. When they had descended, then they went to bathe—the ruler and the lords. Thus did they do penance at night.

For four days they fasted, with faces veiled in fasting capes. And for as many days, at noon, they offered incense before [the image of] Uitzilopochtli. Likewise, for as many nights, at midnight, they offered incense and made blood offerings before [the image of] Uitzilopochtli, and they bathed themselves.

THIRD PARAGRAPH, in which it is related how they ended the penance, and took the ruler to the courtyard of the palace; and the others they took to their homes.

And after this, when the four days and four nights were ended during which the ruler and lords had fasted and done penance—at that time the ruler came forth, that they might escort him there to the great palace, the ruler's residence. And also at that time the lords entered their homes.

And when this had come to pass, then the ruler chose a propitious day on which the ruler's feast might be observed. He commanded all the major-domos to accord others and give them all capes, and costly devices, and shields.

FOURTH PARAGRAPH, in which it is told how the ruler made summons to a feast.

Then he bade to a feast those from every city. He asked to the banquet the ruler of Michoacan, and the ruler of Cuextlan, and the ruler of Metztitlan, and the lords of the Totonac country, and the lords of Tlaxcala, and the ruler of Cholula, and the lords

Auh iioaltica, in jcoac ioalnepantla oaçic, meoa in tlatoanj, ioan in tecutlatoque, ic ommotlapachoa in neçaoalquachtli: ioan concuj in jntlema ioan icpaxiquipilli in vncan temj copalli, ioan vitztli, ioan conmocactia in jmpoçolcac: auh in iehoantin teupixque papaoaque, qujntlacoaantiuj, in qujujca, icpac vitzilopuchtli, injc ommjço iooalnepantla, ioan ontlenamaca oncopaltema, in jxpan vitzilopuchtli.

çan no iuj oaltemo tecpantiujtze, qujntlacoaana in teupixque papaoaque, ic ixtlapachiuhtiuj in neçaoalquachtli omjcallo, in ooaltemoque, njman ic huj in maltizque, in tlatoanj, ioã tecutlatoque, injc iooaltica tlamaceoaia,

naujlhujtl in moçaoaia ic ixqujmjliuhticatca in neçaoalquachtli, auh izqujlhujtl in nepãtla tonatiuh, in ontlenamacaia ixpan vitzilopuchtli: çan no izqujioal, in ioalnepantla tlenamacaia, ioan onmjçoa in jxpan vitzilopuchtli, ioan maltiaia.

INJC EY PARRAPHO: ipan mjtoa, in quenjn qujtzonqujxtiaia tlamaçeoaliztli, ioan qujujcaia in tlatoanj, in tecpan itoalco: ioã in oc cequjntin qujnujcaia in jnchan.

Auh in ie iuhquj in otzonqujz naujlhujtl, ioan nauhioal, in oonmoçauh, in ontlamaçeuh tlatoanj, ioan tecutlatoque, qujnjcoac qujça in tlatoanj, injc concaoa in vmpa vei tecpan tlatocan. Auh in tecutlatoque, qujn no icoac calaquj in jnchan.

Auh in ie iuhquj: njman ic qujpepena in tlatoanj, in qualli tonalli, in jpan motlatocapacaz, qujnnaoatia, in jxqujchtin calpixque, in jxqujch tilmatli, ioan tlaçotlanquj tlaujztli, ioan chimalli, in qujtetlauhtiz, in qujtemacaz.

INJC NAUJ PARRAPHO, vncan mjtoa, in quenjn qujchioaia tecoanotzaliztli, in iehoatl tlatoanj.

Niman ic tecoanotza, in noujian altepetl ipan, qujcoanotza in mjchoacan tlatoanj, ioan cuextlan tlatoanj, ioan metztitlan tlatoanj, ioan totonacapan tlatoque, ioan tlaxcallan tlatoque, ioan cholollan tlatoanj, ioan uexotzinco tlatoque, ioan tenjtla tla-

of Uexotzinco,[8] and the lords of foreign lands, and the lords of Tzapotlan, and the lords of Anauac, and the ruler of Tehuantepec, and all the lords posted on the shores of the oceans, and all the lords of the cities encircling Mexico—the ruler of Texcoco and the ruler of Tlacopan.

And when all the invited lords had assembled—[both] friendly and unfriendly lords—he provided them food. He gave them drink and food; costly goods he gave them all: capes without price, and valuable breech clouts, and devices, and costly shields. There was dancing; there was a procession; there was singing, night and day, as the ruler provided them solace.

And at that time he also gave gifts to all the noblemen, brave warriors, and lords, and judges, and rulers of the youths, and all the singers, and all the keepers of the gods, fire priests, and [other] priests.

And when the feast ended, then all the bidden guests departed.

FIFTH PARAGRAPH, in which it is told how the ruler adorned himself when he was to war upon some city.

And then, when some days had passed, the ruler proclaimed war—that they would go to set forth somewhere to war. He gave costly devices and shields to the noblemen and to all the brave warriors and men [at arms]. And the ruler himself went to war. To set forth to battle and to conquer, he took all the warriors, and the lords of all the cities about, that they might set forth to war and conquest. And when they had gone forth to conquer and to wage war, they rejoiced greatly over the number of captives whom they had taken, since they would slay them all before [the image of] Uitzilopochtli in order with them to observe his feast. And he accorded honor to all the brave warriors and captors; with many things did he favor them. He gave them costly capes, and breech clouts, and long labrets, and head bands; and he gave them titles by which they would be honored and obeyed as men [at arms] and brave warriors.

toque, ioan tzapotlan tlatoque, ioan anaoac tlatoque, ioan tequantepec tlatoanj: ioan in jxqujchtin tlatoque, ilhujcaatentli qujtztoque, ioan in jxqujchtin tlatoque in altepetl ipan, qujiaoalotoque mexico, tetzcuco tlatoanj, ioan tlacopan tlatoanj.

Auh in jcoac ocenqujzque in jxqujchtin tlacoanotzaltin tlatoque, in jicnihoan tlatoque ioan iiauhoan: njman ic qujntlaqualtia, qujnmaca in atl, in tlaqualli, tlaçotlanquj, qujntlauhtia in jxqujch tlaçotilmatli, ioan tlaçomaxtlatl, ioan tlaujztli, ioan tlaçotlanquj chimalli, netotilo maceoalo, cujco, ceioal cemjlhujtl, in tepaqujltia tlatoanj,

auh in jcoac no qujntlauhtia, in jxqujchtin pipiltin, tiacaoã, ioan tecutlatoque, ioan achcacauhti, ioan telpuchtlatoque, ioan ixqujchtin cujcanjme, ioan ixqujchtin teupixque tlenamacaque, tlamacazque:

auh in otzonqujz tecoanotzaliztli, njman ic ompeoa in jxqujchtin tlacoanotzalti.

INJC MACUJLLI PARRAPHO: vncan mjtoa, in quenjn mocencaoaia, in tlatoanj, injc cana iautiz, altepetl ipan.

Auh çan njman iquezqujlujioc, iaotlatoa in tlatoanj, injc cana iauqujxoalotiuh, qujntlauhtia in tlaujztli tlaçotlanquj ioan chimalli im pipilti, ioan in jxqujchtin tiacahoan, oqujchti: auh iioma in tlatoanj in iauh iauc, in oniaoqujça, in ontepeoa qujujca in jxqujchti iauqujzque, ioan in noujian tlatoque altepetl ipan inic oiaoqujça, ontepeoa: auh in jcoac õtepeoato, oiaoqujçato cenca paquj, in quexqujch malli ocanato, injc mochintin ixpan vitzilopuchtli qujnmjctiaia, inic inca ilhujqujxtiaia. Auh in ixqujchtin tiacaoan, tlamanjme, qujnmaujziotia, mjiec tlamãtli injc qujmjcnelia, qujntlauhtia in tlaçotilmatli, ioan maxtlatl, ioan teçacatl, ioan tlalpilonj, ioan qujntocamaca injc maujztililozque, injc tlacamachozque, injc oqujchti, tiacahoã.

---

8. In *ibid.*, *uexotzinco tlatoque* is followed by *yoan mixtecapan tlatoque*, and rulers of the Mixteca country.

Nineteenth Chapter, in which is described the ordering of the market place, and [how] the ruler took great care of it.

The ruler took care of the directing of the market place and all things sold, for the good of the common folk, the vassals, and all dwellers in the city, the poor, the unfortunate, so that [these] might not be abused, nor suffer harm, nor be deceived nor disdained. Thus were things bought, or sold: they arranged them in order so that each thing sold would be placed separately—in its own place or station. They were not spread about in confusion.

Market place directors were appointed to office. They cared for, and attended to, the market place and all and each of the things sold—the merchandise which was there. Each of the directors took care, and was charged, that no one might deceive another, and how [articles] might be priced and sold.

Separate were those who sold gold and silver, and green stone, and turquoise, and emeralds, and quetzal feathers, and [those of] the blue cotinga, and the red spoonbill, and all the various precious feathers of birds, which were needed for devices and shields.

Separate were those who sold chocolate, aromatic herbs,[1] and vanilla. Apart were those who sold great capes, costly capes, embroidered capes, costly breech clouts, embroidered skirts and shifts, large common capes, maguey fiber capes, and thin maguey fiber capes.

And all food necessary to them also was sold separately: dried grains of maize, white, black, red, and yellow; yellow beans, white ones, black, red; pinto beans; large beans; gray amaranth seed, red amaranth seed, and fish amaranth; white chía,[2] black chía, and the wrinkled variety;[3] salt; fowl; turkey cocks and hens; quail; rabbits, hares, and deer; ducks

Ic caxtolli onnauj capitulo: ipan mjtoa, in tlatecpanaliztli in tianqujzco: auh in iehoatl tlatoanj, cenca qujmocujtlaujaia.

In tlatoanj qujmocujtlaujaia ipan tlatoaia in tianqujztli, ioã ixqujch tlanamactli, impampa cujtlapilli, atlapalli, maçeoalli, ioan ixqujch aoa, tepeoa in jcnotlacatl, in motolinja, injc amo quequeloloz, injc amo xixicoloz, injc amo ica necacaiaoaloz, injc amo nexictiloz, injc motlacouja, in anoço itla qujmonamaqujlia qujtecpanaia, injc nononqua monamacaz, icecentlamantli tlanamactli, çan iieeian, çan ioonoian, amo ixneliuhtoca,

qujmjxquetzaia, in tianqujzpan tlaiacanque, in qujmocujtlaujaia, in jpan tlatoaia in tianqujztli: ioan ixqujch tlanamactli, icecẽtlamantli tlanamactli, tiamjctli, ipan manca, qujmocujtlaujaia cecentlamantin tlaiacanque, in innecujtlaujl catca, injc aiac texixicoz, ioan quenjn tlapatiioaz, quenjn tlanamacoz.

Nonqua onoca in qujnamaca in coztic, ioan iztac teucujtlatl, ioan chalchiujtl, ioan teuxiujtl ioã quetzalitztli, ioan quetzalli, ioã xiuhtototl, ioan tlauhquechol, ioan ixqujch nepapan totoiujtl, tlaçotli in jtech monequja tlaujztli chimalli.

Nonqua onoca in qujnamaca cacaoatl, vej nacaztli, tlilxochitl. Nonqua onoca in qujnamaca veuej tilmatli, tlaçotilmatli, tlamachio tilmatli, tlaçomaxtlatl, tlamachcuejtl, tlamachvipilli, quachtli, ichtilmatli, aiatl,

ioan in ixqujch qualonj, in tetech monequj, no nonqua monamaca, tlaolli iztac, iauhtlaolli xiuhtoctlaolli, coztic tlaolli, coztic etl, iztac etl, tlilletl, chichiltic etl, çolcujcujltic etl, aiecotli. Nexoauhtli, chichiltic oauhtli, mjchioauhtli. Iztac chia, tliltic chiã, chiantzotzol, iztatl: totoli, vexolotl, çiaoatotoli, çoli, tochi, çitli, maçatl, canauhtli, atzitzicujlotl, pipixcan,

---

1. *Vej nacaztli: Cymbopetalum penduliflorum* (Dunal) Baill, in Emmart, *op. cit.*, p. 315.
2. Cf. Chap. 13, n. 23, *supra*.
3. Cf. Chap. 13, n. 21, *supra*. Sahagún (Robredo ed.), III, p. 61, says it is *"una semilla como lentejas blancas."*

and other water birds,[4] gulls,[5] and wild geese;[6] maguey syrup and honey; hot chilis, chili from Atzitziuacan, small chilis,[7] chili powder, yellow chili, chili from the Couixca, sharp-pointed red chilis, long chilis, smoked chilis; small, wild tomatoes,[8] and ordinary tomatoes.

And separately were sold every kind of fruit: the American cherry, avocados, plums, guavas, sweet potatoes, manihot,[9] sapotas,[10] anonas,[11] yellow sapotas, sapotillas,[12] *tejocotes*,[13] tuna cactus, mesquite beans, marchpane, *cacomites*,[14] *cimate* roots,[15] squash cut in pieces, chayote,[16] squash seeds, *Cassia* seeds;[17] and white fish, frogs, and water dogs; water fly eggs, water flies, lake scum, and red shellfish; and white paper made of the bark of trees, and incense, and rubber, and lime, and obsidian; and firewood, and poles, logs, planks, and chips of wood; digging sticks, pointed oaken poles, hatchets, paddles, staves; maguey roots,[18] maguey fiber, and cured leather, and sandals; and copper axes, copper needles, and carpenters' and sculptors' copper chisels; and all manner of edible herbs—onions, water plant leaves, thistles,[19] amaranth greens and heads,[19a] purslane, mixed greens, varieties of sorrel;[20] tuna cactus fruit, sweet and acid; squash greens, tender young squash, squash blos-

tlalalacatl. Necutetzaoac, quauhnecutli, tonalchilli, atzitzioacaiotl chilli, chiltecpin, texiochilli, chilcoztli, coujxcaiotl chillj, mjlchilli, viiac chilli, pocheoac chilli, mjltomatl, xitomatl:

ioan nonqua monamaca, in jzqujtlamantli xochiqualli. Capoli, aoacatl, maçaxocotl, xaxocotl, camotli, quauhcamotli, teçontzapotl, eeiotzapotl, atzapotl, tzapotl, texocotl, nochtli, mjzqujtl, itlaaqujllo, chiancaca, cacomjtl, çimatl, aiotlatlapantli, chaiotl, aiooachtli, quauhaiooachtli, ioan iztac mjchin, cujatl, axolotl, aoauhtli, axaxaiacatl, tecujtlatl, izcaujtli, ioan iztac quauhamatl, ioã copalli, ioan olli, ioan tenextli, ioan itztli, ioan tlatlatilquaujtl, ioan quaoacatl, quammjmjlli, vapalli, tlaxamanjlli, victli, vitzoctli, tlateconj, aujctli, matlaquaujtl, menelhoatl, ichtli, ioan cuetlaxtli, ioan cactli, ioan tepoztli, quauhxelolonj, ioan tepozcoiolomjtl, ioan tepoztli tlacujcujoalonj, ioan tepoztlaquauhicujlolonj, ioan in ixqujch tlamãtli qujlitl qualonj, xonacatl, tzaianalqujlitl, vitzqujlitl, oauhqujlitl, oauhtzontli, itzmjqujlitl, qujllanenel, iztac xoxocoioli, xoxocoiolujujlan, nopalli, xoconochtli, axoxoco, aioiacaqujlitl, aionanacatl, aioxochqujlitl, eçoqujlitl, exotl, elotl, xilotl, ooatl, mjiaoatamalli,

---

4. *Atzitzicuilotl:* "*son redondillas, tienen los picos largos, y agudos y negros; tienen los pies largos; son cenicientes y tienen el pecho blanco; dicen que nacen en la provincia de Anáhuac; vienen a esta Laguna de México entre las aguas o lluvia; son muy buenas de comer. Dicen que éstas, y los tordos del agua, por tiempo se vuelven en peces, dicen que las ven entrar a bandas en la mar, dentro del agua, y que nunca más parecen*" (*ibid.*, p. 170). Cf. also Seler, *Einige Kapitel*, p. 125, n. 1; Cecilio A. Robelo: *Diccionario de Aztequismos* (Cuernavaca: Imprenta del autor, 1904), pp. 542-543. Santamaría, *op. cit.*, I, p. 487 (*chichicuilote*) says there are two species—*Phalaropus wilsonii* BP and *Lobipes lobatus* L.

5. *Pipixcan:* "*son blancas y del grandor de palomas, tienen alto vuelo, críanse hacia la mar, y al tiempo de coger el maíz vienen acá dentro a la tierra; cuando estas aves vienen, entiéndese que es tiempo de coger el maíz*" (Sahagún, *op. cit.*, p. 183). In Santamaría, *op. cit.*, II, p. 485, these are *Larus franklinii* SW & Rich, currently called *apipizca.*

6. *Tlalalacatl:* "*ánsares monciños . . . . grandes como los de España; tienen los pies colorados y el pico, son pardillos; tienen buena carne; tienen debajo plumas blancas y blandas, (y) de estas plumas se aprovechan para hacer mantas; las plumas de encima son recias, tienen buenos cañones para escribir*" (Sahagún, *op. cit.*, p. 169). These (*tlalalacate*), according to Santamaría, *op. cit.*, III, p. 184, are *Anser albifrons* GM.

7. Cf. Chap. 13, n. 22, *supra.*—"*Cierto género de chile llamado chiltecpin, muy tostado y mezclado con ulli*" (Sahagún, *op. cit.*, p. 102).

8. Cf. Chap. 13, n. 20, *supra.*

9. Cf. Chap. 13, n. 10, *supra.*

10. Cf. Chap. 13, n. 7, *supra.*

11. Cf. Chap. 13, n. 8, *supra.*

12. Siméon, *op. cit.;* note also, however, Chap. 13, n. 7, *supra.*

13. *Texocotl:* tejocote—*Crataegus mexicana* Moc. & Ses. (Santamaría, *op. cit.*, III, p. 150).

14. *Cacomitl:* cacomite—*Tigridia pavonia* Kerr; *oceloxóchitl*, of edible root (*ibid.*, I, p. 254). Also Hernández, *op. cit.*, II, p. 657.

15. *Cimatl:* cimate, a condiment (Santamaría, *op. cit.*, I, p. 352). In Hernández, *op. cit.*, II, it is identified as *Desmodium amplifolium* Hemsl. (p. 659) or *D. parviflorum* Mart. y Gal (p. 661).

16. *Chaiotl:* chayote—*Sycios edulis; Sechium edule; Cucumis acutangulus* (Santamaría, *op. cit.*, I, p. 477). In Hernández, *op. cit.*, I, p. 168, *Sechium edule* Sw.

17. In Hernández, *op. cit.*, I, pp. 171ff., various kinds of *quauhayouachtli* are identified as *Jatropha curcas* Linn., *Manihot utilissima* (?) Pohl, *Croton* sp., *Cassia fistula* Linn.

18. *Menelhuatl:* metl (maguey), nelhuayotl (*principio, comienço*, in Molina, *op. cit.*).

19. Emmart, *op. cit.*, p. 213, notes that Siméon must be in error in translating *uitzquilitl* as cardoon, since the latter is not native to Mexico; the *Badianus MS* (Pls. 10, 73) illustrates a thistle (*Cirsium* sp.). Santamaría, *op. cit.*, II, p. 82, describes it (*güisquelite*) as, "*En Méjico especie de alcachofa*" (artichoke).

19a. See Sauer, *op. cit.*, pp. 565-6, 569. Sauer suggests that "*huauhtzontli* may be a corruption of . . . *cuauhtzontli*," a chenopodium: *C. Nuttalliae* and *C. pueblense* are mentioned.

20. *Xoxocoioli:* jocoyol—*Oxalis angustifolia* H. B. K.; *O. corniculata* L.; *O. tetraphylla* Cav.; *O. verticillata* Dc. (Santamaría, *op. cit.*, II, p. 154). Emmart (*op. cit.*, p. 236) mentions other varieties of *Oxalis*, but on p. 213 notes that the term sorrel is used also for *Rumex* (subgenus *Acetosa*), and that *xoxocoyolin* likewise identifies two species of *Begonia*.

soms; bean greens[21] and green beans; green maize, tender maize, tender maize stalks; tamales of maize blossoms, tortillas of green maize, and all edible things—tortillas, tamales, tamales and tortillas with honey, large tortillas, and rolled tortillas.

And also there were proprietors among whom were spread out smoking tubes, pipes, and cigars, [some] quite resinous and aromatic; and tobacco bowls; and large pottery braziers and hearths, and earthen basins, and pots, and jars for storing water, and settling jars, and flat cooking plates, and sauce vessels, and earthen cups, and everything [made of] earthenware.

And those who were directors of the market place, if they did not show concern over their office, were driven forth and made to abandon their office. And if someone sold stolen goods—perchance a costly cape, or a green stone,—if it were made known and he did not declare from whom he had bought that which had been stolen, they went to exact the penalty, and he died. Such was the sentence of the lords and judges, so that [men] would be fearful of that which was stolen and no one would buy it.

It was the duty of the market place folk to make the war provisions—biscuits, and finely ground, dried maize and chía seeds, and dried maize dough, and dried, lime-treated maize dough. With these was the market place charged, and the market place directors, the men and women thus appointed, were charged with assigning the tribute.

elotlaxcalli, ioan in jxqujch qualonj, tlaxcalli, tamalli, necutamalli, necutlaxcalli, vei tlaxcalli, tlaxcal-mjmjlli.

No ioan vncatca, in tlaiacanque in jpan manca acaquaujtl, acaiietl, iietlalli, vel ocotzoio, ioan xochiocotzotl, ioan iiecaxitl, ioan apantlecaxitl, ioã tlequaztli, ioan apaztli, ioan xoctli, ioan atlalilcomjtl, ioan xaiocomjtl, ioan comalli, ioan molcaxitl, ioan in çoqujtecomatl, ioã in jxqujch tlamantli çoqujtlatqujtl.

Auh in iehoantin tianqujzpan tlaiacanque, intlacamo qujmocujtlauja, intequjuh, totoco, ioan caoaltilo in jntequjuh. Auh intla aca tlachtectli qujnamaca, aço tlaçotilmatli, anoço chalchiujtl, intla oiximachililoc, intlacamo qujnextiz in aqujn qujcohujli, in tlein tlachtectli, qujtzacutiuh, mjquja, iuhquj tlatzontequjliaia, in tlatoque, tecutlatoque, ic mjmacaçia in tlein tlachtectli, aiac vel qujcoaia,

in jntequjuh catca tianqujzpantlaca qujchioaia iiaujtacatl, in tlaxcaltotopochtli, ioan pinolli, ioan texoatzalli, ioan nextamalhoatzalli, injc ipan tequjtia tianqujztli, ioan tianqujzpan tlaiacanque, in tlaixquetzalli oqujchti, ioan çioa in tequjtlatoque catca.

21. Sahagún, *op. cit.*, p. 235, describes *eçoquilitl* as *"hojas y ramas de los frijoles"*; on p. 338, however, it is given as *Mesembryanthemum blandum* L.

Twentieth Chapter, in which is told how they reared the sons of lords and noblemen.

And here is described the rearing of the sons of those who were lords, and of all the princes, who were the sons[1] of lords and noblemen.

Their mothers and fathers nourished and raised them, or nursemaids raised them while they were still small children.

And when they could run, when they were perhaps six years old, thereupon [the boys] went [forth] to play. Their pages—perhaps two, or three—accompanied them that they might amuse them. [The child's] father or mother charged these [pages] that [the boy] not behave ill, that he not taint himself with vice, as he went along the streets.

And also they took great care that he should converse fittingly with others—that his conversation should be proper; that he should respect and show reverence to others—[when] perchance he somewhere might chance to meet a judge, or a leading militia officer, or a seasoned warrior, or someone of lesser rank; or a revered old man, or a respected old woman; or someone who was poor. He should greet him and bow humbly. He said: "Come hither, my beloved grandfather; let me bow before thee." And the old one who had been greeted then said: "O my beloved grandson, O precious necklace, O precious feather, thou hast shown me favor. May it go well with thee."

And when the young boy thus saluted others, they praised him highly for it. They rejoiced greatly over it; they were joyful because of it. They said: "How will this beloved child be, if he shall live? He will in sooth be a nobleman. Mayhap his reward will be something [great]."

And when he was already maybe ten, twelve, or thirteen years old, they placed him in the priests' house; they delivered him into the hands of the fire priests and [other] priests, that he might be reared

Ic cempoalli capitulo: vncan mjtoa, in quenjn qujnoapaoia in inpilhoan tlatoque, ioan pipilti.

Auh njcan mjtoa: in jnneoapaoaliz in iehoantin in tlatoque impilhoan, ioan in jxqujchtin in tlaçopipilti, in jnpilhoan tlatoque, pipilti.

iehoantin in jnnaoan, in jntaoan qujmjzcaltia, qujnoapaoa, anoço chichioame in qujnoapaoa in oc pipiltotonti:

auh in jcoac ie uel nenemj, aço ie chiquacenxiuhtia, njman ie ic iauh in maaujltiz, in qujnujca ixolooa aço ome anoço ei in caaujltiz, iehoantin qujncocultia in jtatzin in jnantzin injc amo tlauelilocatiz, injc amo qujmocujtlaujz tlauelilocaiotl: in jcoac otli qujtocaz.

Auh no cenca qujcujtlaujltiaia injc vel tenotzaz, injc qualli iez in jtlatol, injc teimacaçiz, injc temauhcaittaz, aço cana qujnamjqujz aço tecutlato, anoço achcauhtlaiacati, anoço iautequjoa, anoço çan aca tlapaltzintli, anoço veuentzin, anoço ilamatzin, anoço aca motolinja, qujtlapaloz cenca mopechteca, qujlhuja, xioalmoujca nocultzine, ma njmjtznotlaxili: auh in iehoatl oqujtlapalo veuentzin njmã qujlhuja noxujuhtzine cozcatle quetzalle otinechmocnelili ma ximonenemjti:

auh injc iuh tetlapaloa, y, in piltontli, ic cenca qujiecteneoa, cenca ic papaquj, ic motlamachtia. qujtoa: quenamj ietiuhi in piltzintli intla nemjz ca tel pilli, aço itla imaçeoal iez.

Auh in jcoac ie matlacxiuhtia aço ie vmome, anoço ie omej, icoac qujcalaquja in calmecac, inmac qujmoncaoaia in tlenamacaque, in tlamacazque, injc vmpa izcaltiloz nonotzaloz, tlachieltiloz inic vel

---

1. After *jnpilhoan*, the *Real Academia de la Historia MS* has the following, omitted from the *Florentine Codex: "Inic mouapaua inic mozcaltia ça ye no yui in omihto in tlacatiliztli çan oc"*—"they were reared and brought up just as hath been told in the [section] on birth."

there, corrected, and instructed; that he might live an upright life. They constrained him to do the penances, setting fir branches [on the city altars] at night, or there where they went to place the fir branches on mountain tops—there where sacrifices were made at midnight. Or else he entered the song house; they left him in the hands of the masters of the youths. They charged him with the sweeping, or with dancing and song—with all which was concerned with the performance of penances.

And when he was already fifteen years old, then he took up arms; or, reaching twenty years of age, then he went forth to war. First [his parents] summoned those who were seasoned warriors. They gave them to eat and to drink, and they gave gifts to all the seasoned warriors. They gave them large, cotton capes, or carmine colored breech clouts, or capes painted with designs. And then they besought the seasoned warriors; in just the same way as hath been told above, so they entreated them.[2]

And then they took him to the wars. The seasoned warriors went taking great care of him, lest somewhere he might be lost. And they taught him well how to guard himself with a shield; how one fought; how a spear was fended off with a shield. And when a battle was joined, when already there was fighting and perhaps already captives were being taken, they taught him well and made him see how he might take a captive. Perhaps then he took a captive with the aid of others, or he [alone] could take one.[3] For truly it was well seen to that many men become brave warriors.

And when captives were being taken, then at once couriers, of marriageable age, quickly went forth, called victory messengers, who speedily went to inform Moctezuma.

And when the victory messengers had come to arrive, then they quickly entered into the presence of Moctezuma and said to him: "O our lord, O my youth, pay thy debt and thy service [to the god]; for the omen of evil, Uitzilopochtli, hath shown favor and been gracious. For they have pierced the rampart of men dexterous in arms of the city against which they have gone. Into it have marched[4] the Mexicans of Tenochtitlan, the Mexicans of Tlatilulco, the Tepaneca, the Acolhua, the Otomí, the Matlatzinca,

nemjz qujcujtlaujltia in tlamaceoaliztli, in ioaltica in acxoiatlaliliztli içaçocampa acxoiatlalitiuh in tepeticpac, in vmpa onmjcoia ioalnepantla, anoce cujcacali qujcalaquja, inmac concaoa in tiachcaoan, qujcujtlaujltia in tlachpanaliztli, anoço cujcoianoliztli, in jxquich tlamantli tlamaçeoaliztli mochioaia.

Auh in jcoac ie caxtolxiuhtia icoac moiaomamachtia anoço açi cempoalxiujtl injc qujça iauc, in iehoantin tequjoaque achtopa qujnnotza qujntlaqualtia. qujmatlitia, ioan qujntlauhtia in jxqujchtin tequjoaque, in qujnmaca aço quachtli anoço nochpalmaxtlatl, anoço tlacujlolli in tilmatli. Auh njman qujtlatlauhtia in tequjoaque, çan ie no iuhquj in omjto tlacpac injc qujntlatlauhtia.

Auh njman ic qujhujca, in iauc: vel qujmocujtlaujtiuj in tequjoaque, in ma cana xiccaoalo: auh vel qujmachtia, in iuh momana chimalli, in iuh iautioa, in iuh mochimaltopeoa mjtl. Auh in jcoac ie mochioa iauiotl, in ie necalioa, anoce ie tlamalo, uel conjttitia, vel contlachieltia, in vmpa tlamaz: aço njmã tepallama, anoço njman vel ic caçi ipampa ca cenca necujtlaujlo ca mjiec tlacatl in jtiacauh mochioa.

Auh in ie tlamalo, njman achtopa oalpeuhtiqujça in tequjtque tlapaliuj, intoca tequjpan titlanti in qujoalnonotztiuetzi motecuçuma:

auh in oacico tequjpan titlanti, njman ic hiciuhca calactiuetzi ipan in motecuçuma qujlhuja. Totecujoe notelpotzine, ma ximotlacotili, ma ximotequjtili, ca oicnopiltic, onmaceoaltic, in tetzaujtl in ujtzilobuchtli, ca otepan qujtopeuh in quauhtenamjtl, in ocelotenamjtl, ca oia in altepetl: in vmpa tlatlamatitiaque in mexica tenochca, in mexica tlatilulca, in tepanecatl, in aculhoa, in otomjtl, in matlatzincatl, iie ixqujch tlalhoacpanecatl in chinampanecatl.

---

2. This reference appears to be a passage found on fol. 20*v* of the *Academia de la Historia MS* but omitted from the *Florentine Codex*. Cf. Seler in *Einige Kapitel*, p. 319.

3. *Vel ic caçi:* the *Real Academia de la Historia MS* has *ce* for *ic*.
4. *Tlatlamatitiaque:* Siméon, *op. cit.—tlatlamantitiui.*

and finally all the people of the uplands and those of the swamp lands."[5]

And Moctezuma said to them: "You have tired yourselves; you have suffered affliction, O men dexterous in war. Rest yourselves. [But] perhaps you only fool me. Let me still behold the truth of your account."

And then he confined them. If the report which they had made were not true, Moctezuma jailed them and did away with them

And there in battle was when captives were taken. When it had come to pass that they went against and conquered the city, then the captives were counted, there, in wooden cages: how many had been taken by Tenochtitlan, how many had been taken by Tlatilulco, and by the people of the swamp lands and the people of the dry lands everywhere. The captives were examined [to determine] how many groups of four hundred were formed.

Those who counted were the generals and the commanding generals. And then they sent messengers here to Mexico. Those who were sent as messengers were seasoned warriors, who informed Moctezuma of the great veracity of the four-hundred count. They brought word of how many groups of four hundred had been made captive.

And then they declared to him how many of the noblemen had won their reward for having made captives; that haply a number [of them] had had their hair shorn as seasoned warriors, or that some [had been made] leaders of the youths. When Moctezuma heard this, he rejoiced exceedingly, because his noblemen had taken captives. And at that time he freed those whom he had cast in jail—the victory messengers—and he gave them gifts along with the others.

And if war should be proclaimed against Atlixco, or Uexotzinco, and if there once again they took captives, they won much glory thereby; Moctezuma accorded them great honor for it. For his noblemen had taken captives, and had gained repute, and had reached the station of nobility—the estate of the eagle and the ocelot warriors. From there they came to rule, to govern cities; and at that time they seated them with [the nobility], and they might eat with Moctezuma.

Auh qujmjlhujaia in moteçuma, oanqujçiauhque, oanqujhijoujque in oçeloqujchtle: ximotlalican aço çan annechiztlacahuja, ma oc njcchia in jneltica tlatolli:

auh njman qujmoncaltzaqua intlacamo melaoac tlatolli oqujcaqujtique moteçuma qujntlatlatia qujnpopoloa.

Auh in vmpa iauc in iquac otlamaloc, in ie iuhquj in oia in oompoliuh, altepetl, njman ic mocempoa in mamalti, in vncan oacaltitla quezquj oaxioac in tenochtitlã, quezquj oaxioac in tlatilulco, auh inic noujian cenchinanpanecatl, centlalhoacpanecatl, mocemjtta in mamalti quezqujtzontli omuchiuh.

Jehoantin tlapoa in tlatlacochcalca, in tlatlacatecca: auh njman ic oallatitlanj, in njcan mexico, in oalmotitlanj iehoantin in tetequjoaque, in qujoalnonotza motecuçuma, in ie uel imelaoaca in jcentzontecca, in qujoalitquj tlatolli, in quezqujtzontli omochiuh malli:

auh in qujmelaujliaia in quezqujntin otlacnopilhujque in pipilti in otlamaque, aço cequjntin motequjoacaxima anoce cequjntin telpuchiacati. Jn qujcaquja in motecuçuma cenca ic papaquja ipampa ca ipilhoan in ontlamaque: auh qujnjquac qujnqujxtiaia, in qujncaltzaquaia in tequjpan titlanti qujmõtehoan motlatlauhtia.

Auh intla oalmjtoz iaujotl in atlixco, aço vexotzinco, intla oc ceppa vmpa tlamazque, cenca ic vel panuetzi, ic cenca uel qujmmaujztilia in motecuçuma: ipampa ca ipilhoan in ontlamaque, in onmoteniotique in oconmjiaoaiotique in pillotl in quauhiotl, in oceloiotl, ic oncan in qujça in tlatocati, in qujpachoa altepetl, auh qujnjquac intlan qujntlalia: ytlan tlaqua in motecuçuma

5. *Chinampanecatl:* Sahagún's comment on fol. 53 of Book X of the *Florentine Codex* is descriptive: *"y los de la tierra seca, que son las cercanias de las chinanpas."*

He gave them long, yellow labrets; or curved, yellow lip plugs; or long, blue labrets; or curved, blue lip plugs; or curved, green stone lip plugs; or green stone lip plugs; or lip shafts.[6] Then [he gave them] head bands with two quetzal feather tassels [intertwined] with flint knives [fashioned] of gold and with golden pendants; or head bands with two trupial feather tassels; and cured leather ear plugs; and costly capes—the one [known as] the lord's cape, with the obsidian serpent design; or the ashen gray one with red eyes on the border; or with earthen jars designed in feathers; or with the obsidian arrow step design; and costly breech clouts[7]—perhaps the breech clout with twisted ends, [or] with cotton at the ends—various kinds of costly breech clouts; and devices—perchance [the one with] the quetzal feather comb; or the golden banner; or the yellow Xolotl head; or the golden hood; or the golden conical cap; or the quetzal feather banner; or the obsidian butterfly with quetzal feathers and eyes of gold; and costly shields—perhaps [the one of] the skin [and feathers] of the blue cotinga; or of yellow parrot feathers—verily, all the costly shields. And he gave them stewardships: possibly in two places or in three he gave them [such offices]. For truly they had taken [captives].

And if the ruler should die, from these one was chosen to govern the city. And likewise from these, some were placed in the Tlacxitlan, where they pronounced judgments and meted out death sentences. [These were] the Tlacochcalcatl tecutli, or the Ticociauacatl tecutli, or the Cioacoatl tecutli, or the Tlillancalqui tecutli.[8]

in qujnmaca coztic teçacatl, anoço coztic tenclololli, anoço xoxouhquj teçacatl, anoço xoxouhquj tenclololli, anoço chalchiuhtencololli, anoço chalchiuhtentetl, anoço tlanjtentetl: njman ic quetzallalpilonj teucujtlatica tecpaio, ioan teucujtlatl in jpepeiocio, anoço çaquan tlalpilonj, ioan cuetlaxnacochtli, ioan tlaçotilmatli, iehoatl in tlatocatilmatli in jtzcoaio, anoço ixnextentlapallo, anoce iujtica tetecomaio, anoço itzmjxicalcoliuhquj, yoan tlaçomaxtlatl, anoçe tzicoliuhquj maxtlatl, aiacaichcaio, içaço quexqujch tlaçomaxtlatl, ioan tlaujztli, aço quetzalpatzactli, anoço teucujtlapanjtl, anoço tozquaxolotl, anoço teucujtlaquacalalatli, anoçe teucujtlacopilli, anoço quetzalpanjtl, anoçe itzpapalotl quetzallo teucujtlatl in ixtelolo, ioan tlaçochimalli, aço xiuhtotoieoatl, anoçe tozeoatl in ie uel ixqujch tlaçotlanquj chimalli, ioan qujnmaca calpixcantli, aço ooccan, anoço eexcan in qujnmaca: ipampa ca nel ocaçique.

Auh intla mjqujz tlatoanj: iehoantin ceme analoia, injc iehoantin qujpachozque altepetl. Auh çan no iehoantin, cequjntin ontlalilo tlacxitlan, in vncan tecutlatoa, in tlatzontequj, in qujtzõtecticate mjqujztli: tlacochcalcatl tecutli, anoço ticociaoacatl, tecutli, aço çioacoatl tecutli, anoço tlillancalquj tecutli.

---

6. *Tlanjtentetl:* Seler, *op. cit.,* p. 332, has *tlamintentetl.*

7. After *yoan tlaçomaxtlatl,* the *Real Academia de la Historia MS* has the following, omitted from the *Florentine Codex: quaxoxomaxtlatl— Kahlkopfschambinde,* according to Seler, *op. cit.,* p. 332.

8. A passage omitted from the *Florentine Codex* but included in the *Real Academia de la Historia MS,* ending this chapter, has been placed in Appendix B.

Twenty-first Chapter, in which is told how all arose through the ranks until they became judges.

And behold how began the life of the young boy. At first, while still a small boy, his hair was shorn. And when he was already ten years old, they then let a tuft of hair grow on the back of his head. And when he was fifteen years old, then the tuft of hair became long. [This was] when he had nowhere taken captives.

And if he took a captive with the help of others —perchance doing so with the aid of two, or of three, or of four, or of five, or of six, at which point came to an end [the reckoning] that a captive was taken with others' help—then the lock of hair was removed. And thus was the division of their captive: in six parts it came. The first, who was the real captor, took his body and one of his thighs—the one with the right foot. And the second who took part [in the capture] took the left thigh. And the third took the right upper arm. The fourth took the left upper arm. The fifth took the right forearm. And as for the sixth, he took the left forearm.

And when the tuft on the back of his head was removed, he was shorn so that he was left [another] lock: his hair dress kept, on the right side, the hair hanging low, reaching the bottom of his ear; to one side [only] was his lock of hair set. When this [was done], he assumed another face, he appeared otherwise, so that it might be seen that he had made a captive with the help of others [and that] the tuft of hair on the back of his head had been removed.

And then his grandfather, or his beloved uncle, addressed him. He said to him: "My beloved grandson, the sun, the lord of the earth, hath washed thy face. Thou hast taken another face; and thou hast gone to throw thyself against the foe. Let them take thee if, without profit, once more thou takest a captive with the aid of others. What wouldst thou be? Wouldst thou have a young girl's lock of hair? Take care lest thou again take a captive with others' help. Cast thyself against our foes."

Injc cempoalli oce capitulo, vncan mjtoa, in iuhqujma tlamamatlatl injc tlecoia in jxqujchica tecutlato muchioa.

Auh izcatquj injc ontzinti, inemjliz in telpuchtontli, in iacachto çan oc moquateçonoa in oc piltontli: auh in ie matlacxiujtl icoac mocuexpaltia, auh in caxtolxiujtl, icoac cuexpalchicacpul muchioa in acan tlama.

Auh intla tepal otlama aço oteoncaioti, anoço oteecaioti, anoço otenauhcaioti anoço otemacujlcaioti, anoço otechiquacencaioti vncan tlantica injc tepal tlamalo injc necuexpallaçalo. Auh injc qujmoxexelhuja inmal chiquacecçã qujça. Injc ce vel iehoatl in tlamani quicui in itlac: ioan ce imetz: iehoatl in tomaiauhcãpa tocxi: auh inic teoncaiotia, quicui in topochcopa tometz. Auh inic tehecaiotia: quicui in tomaiauhcampa tahcul. Jnic tenauhcaiotia: quicui in topochcopa tacul. Jnic temacuilcaiotia: quicui in tomaiauhcampa tomatzotzopaz. Auh inic tlachiquacencaiotia iehoatl quicui in topochcopa tomatzotzopaz.

Auh in in icoac mocuespallaça, inic moxima motzotzocoltia quioallamachia in innexin imaiauhcãpa quioalhuilancaiotia inacaz itzintlan oalaci iioca motema initzotzocul: in icoac y oc centetl quicui inixaiac oc centlamantli ic tlachia inic ittoz ca otepallama omocuespallaz.

Auh niman ic quitlatlauhtia in icul anoço itlatzin quilhuia. Nosuiuhtze omitzmixamili in tonatiuh, ī tlaltecutli ocentetl ticcuic in moxaiac, auh ça otia, inuicpa xonmomaiaui ma mitzuicacan in toiauoã intla nen oc ceppa tepal xitlama tle tiez cuis timatzotzocoltiz, ma nen ie no cuel tepal titlama ça inca ximomotla in toiauhoan.

And he who took no captive with others' help when, perchance, he had returned three or four times to the wars, they called "Big tuft of hair over the back of the head." And if this was so said of him, he was much ashamed of it. Wherefore he cast himself [into the fray] in order to take a captive with others' aid.

And if he made a captive with the help of others, then his head was pasted with feathers. And he who then did not take a captive with the aid of others might not remove his lock of hair; neither was his head pasted with feathers. Thus was his hair shorn: it was cut like a ring-shaped carrying pad; they shaved only the crown of his head. And for this one, perhaps worldly goods and riches were his lot or he was only poor. And when the tuft of hair on the back of his head had been removed, this one never took and never did they place upon him, an embroidered cape, [but] only white was his small maguey fiber cape, white his small breech clout.

And he who had acted indeed alone and had taken captives, if he took one, was therefore named a leading youth and a captor. And when this came to pass, then they took him before Moctezuma, there at the palace. And by his command he was then stained with yellow ochre; his face was colored with red ochre. They applied it to all of his face. And the majordomos of Moctezuma anointed his temples with yellow ochre.[1]

And at that time Moctezuma granted him favors; he gave him an orange cape with a striped border and a scorpion design to bind on, and a carmine colored breech clout with long ends, and a breech clout of many colors.[2] And then he began to wear capes with designs.

And when he had taken two, likewise they took him there before Moctezuma, at the palace, and likewise his gifts were provided as hath been told.

And when he captured three, likewise his gifts were provided, and he took [the office] of, and they established him as, a master of the youths, a leading youth. He entered a place of dignity, the young men's house, there to nurture and rear [them]. There he reared the young men, there where there was song and dance at night, there in the song house.

Auh in aquin amo tepallama in aço ic espa anoço ic nappa yloti in iaoc quitocaiotia cuespalchicacpul auh in iuh ipan mitoa y ic pinaoa, quinicoac teca momotla inic tepallama.

Auh intla tepal otlama icoac mopotonia, auh in aquin çan niman amo tepallama, amo uel mocuespallaça amono mopotonia, inic moxima moquaiaoalxima çaniio in icoanepantla quichichiqui. Auh ini aço ie imaceoalti in tlalticpacaiotl, in necuiltonolli, auh anoço çan motolinia auh in omocuespallaz aic tle quicui, aic tle itech quitlalia tlamacho tilmatli çan oc ce in iztac in ichtilmaton iztac in imastlaton,

auh ĩ aquin uel oquimiscaui otlama in oce cacic ic motocaiotia telpochiiaqui tlamani. Auh in iquac y quinicoac ispan quiuica in motecoçoma in umpa tlatocān. Auh itencopa inic motecuçauhtiltia mistlapalhoatzalhuia quicemaquia in ixaiac, auh in icanaoacan quitecozauhuia in icalpiscahoan motecuçoma.

Auh quinicoac quitlauhtia in motecuçoma in quimaca camopaltenoaoanqui ioan centetl colotlalpilli ioan centetl nochpalmastlatl iacauiac ioan centetl centzonmastlatl tlatlapalli, auh icoac compeoaltia in tlacuiloltilmatli quiquemi.

Auh inic ome caci çan no vmpa quiuica in ispan motecuçoma in tlatocan auh çan no iuhquj in inetlauhtil mochioaia in omito.

Auh inic ei caci çan ie no iuhqui in inetlauhtil mochioa, auh oncan canaia in quitiachcauhtecaia in telpochiiaqui quicalaquiaia inuehican in telpochcali inic vmpa tlacaoapaoa tlacazcaltia vmpa quimizcaltia in telpopochti, on cuicoianooaia in ioaltica in vmpa cuicacali.

---

1. Following *quitecozauhuia*, the *Real Academia de la Historia MS* has *yuan ompa quimpotonia*—and there they pasted feathers on their heads. This passage is missing in the *Florentine Codex*.

2. The corresponding Spanish text reads: *"vna manta con vnas listas labradas de color morado: y otra manta labrada, de otros ciertos labores de colorado que se llamaua colotlapalli: y . . . vn mastle labrado de colorado, largo que estuujesse bien colgado, y otro mastle labrado de todas colores."*

And when he took four, Moctezuma then let his hair be cut like that of a seasoned warrior. He was named a seasoned warrior. And then also he assumed the titles of a seasoned warrior—perchance Mexicatl tequiua, or Tolnauacatl tequiua, or Ciuatecpancatl tequiua: all the titles of a seasoned warrior. And then in truth was when they placed him on the mat and stool of the warriors' house—there where were gathered the great, brave warriors, where were the Tlacochcalcatl, the Tlacateccatl, the Ticociauacatl, the Atempanecatl—those who were great captains, who had long labrets, who had leather ear plugs, who had head bands with [two] eagle-feather tassels, with which [their hair] was bound.

And if six, or seven, or ten Huaxtecs, or barbarians,[3] were taken, he gained thereby no renown. For this his title was only seasoned warrior.

Then if he went to take captives at Atlixco, or Uexotzinco, or Tliliuhquitepec, for the fifth one whom he captured, then he gained great honor. For this his name was that of a great, brave warrior—a great captain. Then Moctezuma gave him a long, blue labret and a head band with [two] tufts of [eagle] feathers,[4] perchance with silver flint knives [between the eagle feathers], and leather ear plugs, and a bright red, rich, netting cape. And also he was then given a cape of two colors divided diagonally, and a leather cape.

And if he went to take two [captives] from Atlixco or[5] Uexotzinco, then already he filled everyone with awe. Then they gave him a long, yellow labret; he required[6] both the blue [and the yellow] long labrets.[7]

End

Auh inic naui caci ieh icoac quitequioacaxima in motecuçoma motocaiotia tequioa, auh no icoac compeoaltia in tequioacatocaitl aço mexicatl tequioa, anoço tolnaoacatl tequioa anoço cioatecpanecatl tequioa in isquich tequioacatocaitl, auh uel icoac contlalia impetlapan icpalpan in quauhcali in vmpa cenquiztoque in ueuei tiacahoan in vmpa cate in tlacochcalcatl in tlacateccatl in ticociaoacatl, tocuiltecatl, atenpanecatl, iehoantin quauhiaca i, tēçacaoaque cuetlasnacochique quauhtlalpiloni inic ontlalpiloque.

Auh intla chiquacen intla chicome anoço matlactin oquimacic cuestecatl, aço tenitl amo ic panuetzi, çan ic itoca in iaotequioa

ca quinicoac intla otlamato atlisco anoco Uexotzinco, anoço tliliuhquitepec inic macuilli caci icoac vel panuetzi inic veitiacauh in itoca quauhiacatl niman quimaca in motecuçoma xoxouhqui tēçacatl ioan tlalpiloni aço iztac teucuitlatl in itecpaio, ioan cuetlasnacochtli ioan chichiltic cuechintli. Auh no icoac maco in tilmatli chicoapalnacazminqui, ioan cuetlastilmatli.

Auh intla ome cacitiuh in atlisco anoco vexotzinco ie ic centlamamauhtia icoac quimaca in coztic tēçacatl iiomesti quititlani in xoxouhqui tēçacatl.

fin

---

3. *Tenitl:* "Estos tales así llamados [Olmeca, Uixtotin, Mixteca] *están hacia el nacimiento del sol, y llámanles también* tenimes, *porque hablan lengua bárbara*"—Sahagún, *op. cit.*, III, p. 133. Cf. also corresponding Spanish text.

4. Following *tlalpiloni*, the *Real Academia de la Historia MS* has *quauhtlalpiloni*—head band with eagle feather pendants. This word is omitted in the *Florentine Codex.*

5. *Anoco* should be read *anoço.*

6. *Quititlani:* a marginal gloss in the *Real Academia de la Historia MS* suggests that the term is translated *usar.* Cf. also corresponding Spanish text, and, in Siméon, *op. cit., itlani, itlania, itlanilia.*

7. Following *xoxouhqui*, the *Real Academia de la Historia MS* has *in coztic;* these words are omitted in the *Florentine Codex.*

A passage left out of this codex is included in the *Real Academia de la Historia MS*, ending the chapter. It is placed in Appendix C.

APPENDICES

Appendix A

Continuation of the Fourth Paragraph, Chapter Fourteen[1]

In the priests' house of Mexico, there were established and congregated all the keepers of the gods, the fire priests, and [other] priests, the city's devout ones. There they waited [lest] perchance the ruler might require something—perhaps inquire about something, mayhap of something they had seen in all the places where debts [of sacrifice] had been paid upon the mountains and upon the water; there where, afar, were the small pyramids where each night they performed penances.

For these who were fire priests and other priests, when they came forth well into the night, and when, as was said, the shell trumpets were newly blown, first drew their blood before the devil, with thorns, the spines of the maguey; then each one separately set forth, going quite naked. They went [out] having put about them only their pouches with cords,[2] which went filled with dyed, powdered tobacco— this tobacco mixed with a black [dye]—which they chewed as they went. And one proceeded taking with him an incense ladle in which fire went enclosed; and a small cotton bag in which was incense; and pine wood; and he carried his fir branches in his arms, as well as his spines covered with blood, and a shell as his trumpet. And even though it rained hard or was freezing, just so he went.

When he reached whatsoever mountain he was to perform his due upon, then and there he paid his debt [of sacrifice]. He offered incense; he spread out his fir boughs, his bloodied maguey spines. He listened for the time when trumpets were to be sounded in Mexico, at midnight. And when the trumpets had been sounded in Mexico at midnight, then the priests, they who did penance, blew trumpets everywhere there upon the mountains where they paid their debts. Then they turned back, sounding trumpets as they went, in the dawn, when they again entered the priests' house.

Calmecac, mexico, vncan tecpanoaya, vncan mocenquixtiaya in ixquichtin teupixque yn tlenamacaque, yn tlamacazque yn itlamaceuhcauan catca altepetl, conchiaya yn aço itla ic quintemoz tlatoani, aço itla ic tlatlaniz, aço itla quitta yn ompa yzquican omoxtlauha yn tepeticpac, yoã atlan, yoan yn ompa veca caca momoztli, yceceyoual yc tlamaceua.

Ca y iehoanti tlenamacaque, tlamacazque catca yquac quiçaya yn tlaquauhtlapoyaua, ỹ mitoaya yancujcan tlatlapitzalo, achto miçoya in ixpan tlacatecolotl yca vitztli, ỹ metl yuitzo, niman ceceyaca quiçaya, çan petlauhtiuja, çan ixquich onactiuia yn intoxi yntlamecayouh vncan tentiuh yaqualli yehoatl im piçietl tlanelolli tlilli yn quiquatiuja, yoan quitquitiuia tlemaitl tzacuhtiuh vnca yetiuh tletl, yoã xiquipiltontli yc icatiuh copalli, yoã ocotl, yoã quiçiacauia yn iacxoyauh, yoan in iuitz yeheço, yoan tecuciztli yn itlapitzal ỹ manel cenca quiauiz, anoço ceuetziz yuhca viya.

yn iquac yn oacic campa tepetitech tlamatiuh nimã yc vncã moxtlaua, tlenamaca, contema yn iacxoyauh, yn iuitz yeheço, quiualcaqui in queman tlapitzaloz mexico y youalnepantla, auh yn otlapitzaloc mexico youalnepantla, niman yc nouian tlapitza yn tlamacazque yn tlamaceuhque yn ompa tepetitech in campa omoxtlaua, niman valmocuepa tlatlapitztiujtze ye tlatuinauac, y ualcalaqui calmecac.

---

1. See note 11, Chapter 14.

2. Leonhard Schultze Jena, in *Gliederung des Alt-Aztekischen Volks in Familie, Stand und Beruf* (Stuttgart: W. Kohlhammer Verlag, 1952), p. 330, says of the form *totoxi:* "*Da es im Text diejenigen bezeichnet, die den Copalbeutel tragen, wird es sich um Priester handeln.*" The term *tlamecayotia* he translates (*ibid.,* p. 161), "*schliesst sie mit einer Schnur.*"

And if the ruler learned that a fire priest or [another] priest lived in concubinage, and had looked upon a woman, he then pronounced judgment upon him and proceeded to visit punishment upon him. He was despoiled of his goods; they were secreted in his house, [so that] nothing[3] was to be seen [of them]. Likewise judgment was pronounced upon a fire priest or [other] priest if he was drunk.

Auh yn tlatoani yntla quimachiliz, tlenamacac, tlamacazqui omomecati, oquitac çiuatl, niman quitlatzontequilia, quitzacuhtiuh, namoelo, tlatataco yn icha, atl neneçi. ça no yuh tlatzontequililoya yntla otlauan tlenamacac, tlamacazqui.

---

3. *Atl:* probably *atle* is meant.

Appendix B

Continuation of the Twentieth Chapter[1]

... Then were rewarded the seasoned warriors who had brought word of the great veracity of the four-hundred count.[3]

And in this wise the messengers entered; if the flesh of men had been taken captive, it was thus soon made known—all came tying and binding their hair, for the flesh of men had been taken and they thus made it evident. And much did the common folk rejoice when the saw them [and noted] that they came binding [their hair]. They said: "And so[4] the flesh of men hath been taken captive; for all the messengers go with bound [hair]!" And if some came separate [from the others], and came no more with their hair tied and bound, but went with it quite loose, thus they made it known that [our men] had been made captive and that there had been losses in the war. And when the common folk saw them, then a cry of grief arose. Then they said: "And so[4] there have been losses!"

And the noblemen, when they had taken some captives, did not anoint themselves with yellow but rather stained themselves with red ochre, which they put on all over; and they were pasted with eagle down. And Moctezuma rewarded them all with princely capes and breech clouts of great value and high honor, and with preciously wrought quetzal feather devices [ornamented] with gold, and with shields with, perhaps, quetzal feather garlands—very rich shields.

And if one's captives came alive, then he had stewards guard them, and they took great care of them lest they take sick; perhaps it might be twenty or forty that they would guard.

And at the time when the captive was to die, then

... in iquac motlauhtia tequiuaqz,[2] y uel ymelauaca i ye ycentzontecca, oquiualitq'qz tlahtolli.

Auh inic ualcalaquia in titlanti intla otonacatlamaloc. ic monestitiuitze mochintī quihcuistiuitze in inquatzō ontlalpihtiuitze. ypampa ca otonacatlamaloc. ic quitemachitiaya. Auh cenca ic pahpaqz im maceualti in q'mittaya. in ontlacuistiuitze. quitoua. anca otonacatlamaloc ca mochintin ontlacuistiui in titlanti. auh intla ceq'ntin ic xeliuhtiuitze in aocmo ontlalpihtiuitze, y aocmo. yhcuistiuitz inquatzō y ça tontiuh. yc quinestiaya. ca otlamaloc, yuan omicouac ȳ yaoc. Auh in oq'mittaqz maceualtin nimā ic tlachoquiztleua. niman iuh quitoua, anca omicouac.

auh im pipilti in iquac tlaotlamahqz. amo motecoçauhaltia, çan tlauhtica mohçaya quicemaqz in nouia intech. auh mopotonia quauhtlachcayotica. auh in q'ntlauhtia moteccuiçoma moch yeuatl in tlatocatilmahtli. in tlatocamastlatl. y cēca tlaçotli immauizço. yuan tlaçotlanq' quetzallauiztli teocuitlayo. yuan chimalli. aço quetzalcozcayo y uel tlaçotli chimalli.

auh ȳ yeoatl ymal intla oualyoltia niman q'mpieltia in calpisqz uel quimocuitlauia inic amo cocolizcuiz intla oc cempoualtiz anoçoc ompoualtiz. in q̄piezque.

Auh i ye yquac miquiz malli. ȳ yehuatl tlamani

1. See ending of Chapter 20, above.

This passage originally, in the *Real Academia MS*, completed the section ending *titlanti qujmōtehoan motlatlauhtia*. The remaining part of Chapter 20 there appears as an interpolation.

2. The abbreviation for the ending *-que* in the original resembles *-qz*, and is thus reproduced here.

3. This phrase appears capable of more than one interpretation: cf. Molina, *op. cit., tlatzontequilia*, and *centlatzon tequilia*. Seler's translation of a similar passage in Chapter 20 (*Einige Kapitel*, p. 331)—*iye uel y melauaca inicentzontecca*—is "*in richtiger Weise die Zahl der Vierhunderte*."

4. *Anca*: cf. Angel María Garibay K.: *Llave del Náhuatl* (Otumba, Méx.: [Imprenta Mayli], 1940), p. 108; also Horacio Carochi: *Arte de la lengva mexicana* (México: Imprenta del Museo Nacional, 1892), p. 519.

Moctezuma presented the captor a device [with] quetzal feather cups so that possessing it he might slay him as a sacrifice. It did not belong to him; but having it he slew the victim, and he danced with it. He had his rattle stick with him, or the obsidian butterfly or quetzal feather cup [device] set with gold, which he carried upon his back. Possessing it, he slew him as an offering.

And the captive he then took there where he was to die, upon the round sacrificial stone; he proceeded to take the captive by the head, and lead him up to where they would stripe the captive; left him in the hands of one known as the Old Bear. The captives arrived in his care; he made them like his sons. And then [the Old Bear] gave the striped one his four pine cudgels which he would hurl [at his adversaries]. And he gave him his shield and his war club—not edged with obsidian blades but only pasted with feathers.

And those who striped [the captive] were the fire priests and the [other] priests. And the captor remained standing below; he stood regarding his captive. He who died was directly before him.

And after this, when the Old Bear had arrayed the captive, thereupon he went, and gave him to drink wine which was called the gods' wine. He took it to him in a bowl edged with feathers and a sucking tube therein. When [the victim] had drunk, then [the Old Bear] raised [the wine] in dedication [toward] where the sun came forth. So he did with all the shields and war clubs; he raised all of them as offerings, which he gave the captive. When the Old Bear had offered the captive [wine] and made him drink it, thereupon the slayer of the sacrificial victim went forth in order to stripe him. [He had] his shield and his war club edged with obsidian blades and covered with feathers.

And when he had drunk, then he struck at the captive, who likewise struck back. And if the captive were of stout heart, if he were verily a chieftain, really manly, perhaps three or four men fought him. Then, when he fell, they indeed slew him as a sacrifice. And if he were not manly, not a chieftain, then he cast himself there on the round sacrificial stone, and did not fight. Forthwith was he stretched *out upon* his back, and then they gashed open his breast, seized his heart, and raised it in dedication there [toward] where the sun came forth.

nimã ye ic quimaca im moteccuiçoma in tlauiztli quetzalcomitl inic ypan tlamictiz. amo uel ytech pouia çan ipan tlamictia. ypan mitotia ychicauaz yetiuh. anoço itzpapalotl. anoço quetzalcomitl teocuitlayo in q'mama in ipan tlamictia.

auh i yeuatl malli. niman ic quiuica in ompa miquiz temalacac icpac cantiuh contlehcauia, in oncan q'uahuanazqz malli. ymac concaua ytoca cuitlachueue. in imac onacitimanca mamalti iuhq'nma ypilhuã quinchiuaya. Auh niman cõmaca ỹ yocotzonteuh nauhtetl inic q'momotlaz tlauauanq'. yuan q'maca ychimal ymacquauh. amo tenitzyo çan tlapotonilli.

Auh y yeuantin in teuauanaya in tletlenamacaqz in tlamacazqz. auh in tlamani çam moquetzticac tlatzintlan quitzticac in imal. uel ispã im miq'.

Auh ỹ ye iuhqui in oq'cencauh malli in cuitlachueue, niman ye ic yauh quitiz in octli mihtouaya teooctli. inic quitq' acatecomatl tlatempotonilli. in õya. niman ic coniaua in ompa ualquiça tonatiuh mochi iuh q'chiua in chimalli im macquauitl moch coniaua. inic cõmaca malli. auh in oconiti cuitlachueue. niman ye ic yauh in tlamicti inic q'uauanaz ychimal ymacquauh yetiuh tenitzyo tlapotonilli

auh in õya. niman ic cõuiteq' im malli. auh no q'ualhuitequi auh intla yollo chicauac im malli intla uel tiacauh y uel oq'chtli. aço yey tlacatl anoço naui tlacatl in q'moyehecultia. q'niquac uel q'mictia in ouelhuetz. auh intlacamo oq'chtli intlacamo tiacauh çan niman õmoteca in oncan temalacac amo ontlaehecoua. çan iciuhca ommaquetztiteca niman ic conelteq' concuilia in iyollo coniauilia in tonatiuh. ompa ualq'ça

And after the sacrifice was offered, thereupon the stripers who had slain [the victim] — these were the priests — each one danced with the head [of a captive], each one grasping a head [in his hand]. The Old Bear wept at this; he wept for his sons who had died.

And the captive[s] they then flayed; when it was dawn they were already flayed. [They] stood wearing [their] skins. Of each captive who died, their skins were all worn. Then they assembled at Yopico, in the courtyard of the devil. They had their shields, their war clubs, and their rattle sticks. And also came together the great chieftains, the battle-drunk, all important personages. With them were their staves; the pine staves lay in their hands, and they went carrying them.

And when deep night was overspread, they did not take upon their wrists their shields, but took only their staves, as they awaited the time that the sun would burst forth. And when he came forth, thereupon the *tototecti* placed themselves in order — verily, all of them. And the chieftains, upon this, also placed themselves in order and contended against the *tototecti*. Perhaps they faced each other in the four directions. And then the chieftains started forth and fell upon the *tototecti*; they pinched their navels. Very swiftly they pinched them, and then they took after them and went skirmishing with them there in the place where they were, a place called Totectzontecontitlan. There the chieftains turned back; their only task had been to leave them there.

And when this had taken place, thereupon the *tototecti* visited house after house. Nowhere did they omit a house or one's home. Indeed everywhere they entered; and the common folk, seasoned to this, awaited them in order to offer them the things with which they expected them — bunches of ears of maize, tortillas made of uncooked maize, and tamales of maize, amaranth seed, and honey mixed together. For the whole day they went from house to house, [thus treated with] esteem.

And the next day, or [during the next] twenty days, wherever [one of them] went, perhaps in the market place, he begged, and that which he begged he gave to the owner of [the dead] captive. He gave him his share, perchance, of chili, salt, or staves, or pine wood, or grains of maize — all which lay in the market place. Each day [he did] the same.

Auh i ye iuhqui ommicouac. nimã ye ic mihtotia in tlauahuanqz in otemictiqz ȳ yeuantin tlamacazqz. in ipan mihtotia cecentetl in tzontecomatl intlan caana. Auh i yeuatl cuitlachueue. niman ye ic choca q'nchoq'lia ȳ yehuãtin ypilhuã in omicqz.

auh i yeuatl malli nimã ye ic q'xipeua in tlathui ye totec, [çan moquetzticacqui][5] in ieuayo. in isquichtin omicqz mamalti moch onneaquilo in imeuayo. oncan mocenquistia i yopihco in diablo itualco. inchimal immacquauh yetiuh inchicauaztopil. auh no mocenq'stiaya y ueuey tiacauan yetiui. i yaopan miuintiani. uel isquich tlacatl. inquauh yetoc. yeuatl in ocoquauitl immac onoc in quitquitoqz.

oc uel youã im moteca immac tlacuistoqz atle inchimal çanio in quauitl quitq'toqz. quichistimani in quemmã ualquiçaz tonatiuh. auh in oualquiz niman ye ic motecpana in tototecti. uel isq'chtin. Auh in tiacaua nimã ye ic no motecpana q'misnamictimomana in tototecti. aço nauhmapa. in motztimani. auh nimã ye ic ompeua in tiacaua ȳuicpa õuetzi in tototecti q'moncotonilia in inxic ça uel yciuhca in oq'mocotoniliqz nimã ye ic q'ntoca q'micaltiui ompa q'mõmana in innemanaya in itocayocã totectzontecontitlã. oncan ualmocuepa in tiacaua. çan tequitl q'mõcaua.

Auh i ye iuhq' nimã ye ic ui in tepan cacalaquizqz in tototecti. acan quimocauia in calli in techã. uel nouian calaq̃ auh im maceualli ye iuhca īyollo quinchie. in q'mmaca in inchiel. ocholli. uilocpallascalli. ytzocoyouh. nenepanolli. çan cemilhuitl in tepancacalaq' in ontlaçotlalo.

auh in imoztlayoc anoço y cempoualloc. ça campa quiquiça aço tianquizco. tlatlaeuã. in queheua cõmaca im male. q'xelhuia. aço chilli. iztatl. aço quauitl. aço ocotl. anoço tlaolli i ye mochi tianquizco onoc. momoztlae yui.

---

5. This phrase is almost illegible in the original. We have reproduced what the words appear to be.

And when they had come to [the end of] the twenty days, thereupon they went to Yopico. There they laid away their skins; then they cast them down in a cave, a very deep place, and there buried them.

auh in oaciqz cempoualilhuitl nimã ye ic ui i yopihco. ompa quitlalia in imeuayo niman contepeua oztoc uel huecatlã ompa contoca.

Appendix C

Continuation of the Twenty-first Chapter[1]

. . . He alternated [his lip plugs] when he fitted them in. And Moctezuma gave him his head band [with two tufts] of eagle feathers [ornamented] with obsidian knives fashioned of gold, and his cape with, perhaps, the serpent mask design, or the earthen vessel fashioned of feathers, or the ocelot cape with a red border; and a breech clout with long ends, having either the eagle claw or the market place design.

At that time he acquired new sandals—not embroidered nor cut according to a pattern, but black, with their thongs of either orange or red leather. And when he went to the palace, he put the sandals on in order to go along the road. He went receiving great honors, because he was Moctezuma's chieftain. He proceeded with much acclaim. And when he reached the Eagle Gate he drew off the sandals which he had put on; he was no longer shod when he entered the royal palace, where were the great men dexterous in arms, the war leaders.

And also at that time he won the title known as general or commanding general. If the general or commanding general were to die, then [another] would be chosen and selected [from among] those who had been made their deputies. They said that they had become lords of the sun.

And all the seasoned warriors, who had entered the field of battle, all these Moctezuma rewarded. When the Feast of Tlacaxipeualiztli was celebrated, he gave each of them four pieces of black cloth, each eight measures broad. And likewise he gave the leaders of the youths the cape of scorpion design with a striped, orange border and the carmine colored breech clout with the wind jewel design at the ends.

And [as for] those whom we knew to be seasoned war leaders and leaders in the fray, then started [the custom] that Moctezuma [had] the hair of those who were chieftains cut as shorn ones or as Otomí [warriors].

When and wheresoever war was proclaimed, always they remained guarding and paying heed to

. . . q'papatla y' çaço catleuatl conaquiz. auh in iquauhtlalpiaya coztic teocuitlatl in itecpayo. auh in itilma, aço couaxayacayo, anoço yuitica tehtecomayo, anoço ocelotentlapalli in q'maca. moteccuiçoma yuã mastlatl yacauiac aço quauhiztio, anoço tianquiztli ommãtiuh ĩ mastlatl.

yquac yancuicã quicui in cactli, amo tlahmachyo amo cuicuiltic çan tliltic. in icuetlasmecayo aço uitzteculli. anoço chichiltic cuetlastli. auh in iquac ye yauh tecpã ommocactia inic ohtli q'toca. cenca momauizçotitiuh ypampa ca ytiacauh im moteccuiçoma. cẽca motleyotitiuh. Auh i ye onaci quauhquia-uac quicopina in icac quitlalia aoc momocactia inic calaqui tecpan tlahtoca. in ompa cate uehuey qua-quauhti, uehuey ocelome i yaotachcaua.

Auh no yquac quimahceua in tocaitl im mitoua tlacochcalcatl. anoço tlacateccatl. intla miquiz tla-cochcalcatl anoço tlacateccatl yquac ano pepenalo. yeuantin ym ixiptlayouã mochiuaya. quihtouaya ytlahtocaua mochiua in tonatiuh.

Auh in isquichtin i yaotequiuaqz i yaotitlancalaqz i ye mochintin in q'ntlauhtiaya moteccuiçoma. yquac in tequiquistiloya in tlacaxipeualiztli in q'mmacaya tlilpapatlauac chichicuee çotl nanauhmaca. auh no yui in telpochiaqz in q'mmacaya camopaltẽuauanq' colotlalpili nochpalmastlatl yacayecacozcayo.

Auh i yeuantin ĩ in otiq'nteneuhqz i yaotẽquaqz i yaotachcauã. oncã quiçaya in q'nquachiximaya. motecuiçoma anoço quimotõximaya. in tiacauã catca.

in iquac çaçocampa ualmitouaya yaoyotl çã mo-chipa quichisticate quipopouhticate in inquauhyo in

1. See ending of Chapter 21, above.

their estate as men dexterous in war, as men of valor, as chieftains. Thus none, when they went, might take account that they might die. [For] if war were not proclaimed, if they were not to go off to die, none might know for how much time they might live. And if war were proclaimed, then set forth together the assembled men of Mexico. The generals and the commanding generals led them. When they reached the place which they were to conquer, upon the next day they disposed them in battle array.

And there on the battlefield went the shorn ones in pairs. The Otomí [warriors] also went in pairs. If one of the shorn ones died in the fray and if the other of the shorn ones turned tail, then Moctezuma [had an official] take after him. No more might he enter the Eagle House; they kept him shut away in his [own] house. Of no further use was he. And they suspended the shorn one. And in the same way they exacted penalty of Otomí [warriors] if one of them died [in battle] and if the other fled. They took after him; they suspended him as chieftain. And also they deprived him of rank if he showed fear.

All with which they had bedight him—the precious capes and costly breech clouts—no longer could he assume. He might put on only a poor maguey fiber cape or a wretched yucca fiber cape, as he deserved.

And perhaps in a year or two [Moctezuma] remembered him, sought him out, and drew him from his home. And when he went before Moctezuma, thereupon he gave him again the devices, perhaps [ornamented] with quetzal feathers or with gold. Then [the ruler] gave him gifts; he presented him a bundle of capes, and provided him with grains of maize—he gave him a canoe full or maize grains; and he provided him with *chia*—he weighed out two large measures of *chia*. And thereafter once again he placed himself among [those in] the Eagle House, because he merited once more assuming all the costly capes and breech clouts and all the honors which were his.

And if, as a shorn one, or as an Otomí [warrior], he were to take a captive there at Atlixco or at Uexotzinco, much was Moctezuma's heart gladdened thereby. And all the lords were happy because of it; they were pleased and rejoiced therefor, that those who were their shorn ones or their Otomí [warriors] had taken captives: because men dexterous in war had surrounded [the foe].

imoceloyo inic oquichti inic tiacauā. inic ayac ỹ uiui ça quipopouhtinemi in immiquiz. im ma ualmihto yaoyotl im ma ommiquiti ma oce ontlamati in oc quesquich cauitl nemizqz, auh intla oualmihto yaoyotl nimā cemolini i ye istlacatl mexicatl. in teyacana tlatlacochcalca. tlatlacatecca in oacito in õpa tepeuazqz. oc cemilhuipā ī yaoteca.

auh i ye ompa yaoc. omettitiui in quaquachicti. no omettitiui. in otomi. intla ce oyaomic quachic. intla oc ce ualmocuepa quachiqz. niman ic quitohtocaya ī moteocçoma. aocmo calaqz in q̈uhcali. ça iccen quicallatiaya. aocca moneqz. auh q'caualtiaya inic quachic. Auh çan ye no iuh q'ntlatzacuiltiaya in otomi intla çan no ce omic intla oc ce ualmocuepa. quitohtoca quicauialtia inic tiacauh. auh no quicaualtia inic otlamamauhtiaya.

in isquich in itech oq'tlaliaya in tlaçotilmahtli. in tlaçomastlatl. aoc tle quicui. ça ichtilmahtzintli. anoço icçotilmahtzintli. in q'mulpilia. inic quitlamahceualmacaya.

auh in quilnamiquia aço ce xiuitl anoço õxiuitl. in quitemouaya. ychan in q'ualanaya. auh in õya ispā motecuiçoma. nimā ye ic q'ualmaca in tlauiztli aço quetzallo. anoço teocuitlayo. niman quitlauhtia, cen q'milli in q'maca tilmatli. yuā quitlaoltia cem acalli in q'maca tlaolli yuan quichientia. aço ontetl y uey tzincopinq' ic q'tamachiua chien. auh quī ye no ceppa yquac tetlan motlalia in q̈uhcali. ypampa ca ontlamahceuh oc ceppa mochi q'cui in tlaçotilmahtli in tlaçomastlatl. in isq'ch ytech poui in imauizço.

Auh intla yquachicyo intla yotõyo ypan otlama in ompa atlisco anoço uexotzinco oc cenca ic paquia in iyollo motecuiçoma. yuan in isquichtin tlahtoqz ic papaqz ic motlamachtiaya ic ahauiaya. in oypan tlamahqz inquachicyo in imotõyo. ỹpāpa ca oquimiauayotito in quauhyotl in oceloyotl.

Then were drawn forth and chosen the general and the commanding general. Then the man dexterous in arms attained his end; such honor he won that no one anywhere might be adorned [like him]; no one in his [own] house might assume all his finery. For in truth [because of] his dart and his shield there was drinking and eating, and one was arrayed in cape and breech clout. For verily in Mexico were we, and thus persisted the reign of Mexico.

oncan quiztiuia oncam pepenaloya. in tlacochcalcatl in tlacateccatl mochiuaya. oncan y tlamiani in quhyotl inic p̄auechouaya inic ayac çan campa omochichiuaya. ayac çan icalitic. oquicuic in isquich ynechichiual. ca nel mitl ca chimalli in oyuac in oqualoc. auh in oquemouac in tilmahtli im mastlatl. ca nel mexico in ticate ca ic mani ī mexicayotl.